WILD TOWNS OF NEBRASKA

by

WAYNE C. LEE

THE CAXTON PRINTERS,
Caldwell, Idaho
1992

First printing October, 1988
Second printing May, 1992

Library of Congress Cataloging-in-Publication Data

Lee, Wayne C.
    Wild Towns of Nebraska / By Wayne C. Lee.
    p.   cm.
    Bibliography: p.
    Includes index.
    ISBN 0-87004-325-0 : $14.95
    1. City and town life—Nebraska—History—19 century. 2. Cities
and towns—Nebraska—History—19th century. 3. Frontier and pioneer
life—Nebraska. 4. Nebraska—History, Local. 5. Violence—
Nebraska—History—19th century. I. Title.
F666.L44 1988
978.2′03—dc19   88-20227
                                                              CIP

Printed, lithographed and bound in the United States of America by
The CAXTON PRINTERS, Ltd.
Caldwell, Idaho   83605
156168

WILD TOWNS OF NEBRASKA

Dedicated to:

My wife, PEARL.

Without her many, many hours
of research and typing, this
book would never have been
completed.

And to my sons:

SHELDON and CHARLES,
whose roots will always
be deep in Nebraska,
no matter where they
may live.

Contents

Illustrations

Preface

The stories of wild happenings in the early towns of Nebraska would fill many books of this size. As my research expanded, it became obvious that only a very small number of towns could be included and then only a select number of stories about those towns.

From the start, it was decided to hold the book to a reasonable size so that its price would remain within the means of most readers. To that aim, towns were selected for their individual contributions to Nebraska history—river towns, railroad towns, trail towns and ranch towns.

I could have selected many more towns in each category but the book would have sacrificed manageability. I had to reject towns with wonderful stories and I had to drop many stories from the towns I included because of space limitations.

I hope the towns I have selected will offer the reader a glimpse of the wild side of these early towns and take him on interesting trips into a past that has been almost forgotten.

I discovered during my research that some of the towns with the wildest backgrounds have developed into the fastest growing cities. Perhaps the energy generated in those old days (even if misdirected) carried over to build peaceful thriving communities. Sometimes it is the little boy who singes the hair off the cat who grows up to be president.

Little towns, big towns, wild towns or tame, they have all merged into a state that Nebraskans can be proud of. It is from such rough, sometimes difficult, beginnings that this nation has evolved.

Acknowledgments

Many people helped me in my research of early Nebraska towns but no one more than Ann Reinert, librarian of the Nebraska State Historical Society. She sent me numerous xerox copies of articles and newspaper stories and always had a stack of books ready when I came to the library for research.

Senator Arthur Carmody, of Trenton, certainly one of the most knowledgeable historians in the state of Nebraska, put me on the track of many of the stories in this book. He loaned me books from his private library to help in my research.

Elinor Brown, librarian of the Imperial Public Library, helped me locate hard-to-find books. Anoma Hoffmeister, Chase County historian, also of Imperial, found important articles for me. The late Erma Roller of Champion gave me material that her father, Cornelius Gardner, had researched and written while he was county clerk in the 1930s.

Nellie Snyder Yost, of North Platte, gave me material and loaned me books detailing incidents on North Platte that I could find nowhere else.

Adam and Sarah Hook of Culbertson helped me locate pictures of Culbertson and loaned me several of their own. Mrs. Paul Crews, also of Culbertson, loaned me a picture that I couldn't find elsewhere. Mavis Peterson, librarian of the Culbertson library, provided access to material that was unavailable anywhere else. Mrs. Otis Rogers of Cambridge granted me an interview concerning work her late husband had done in preserving the history of Culbertson.

Emil Elmshaeuser, historian of Ogallala, told me stories of the early town and showed me where to find articles on them. He also gave me some pictures. Elaine Nielsen of Ogallala, who wrote the centennial book for the town, helped me locate many pictures that I needed.

Vance Nelson, curator of the Fort Robinson Museum, spent a day with me, showing me where things happened in Crawford and around the fort, helping me locate items in the museum library and granting an interview that proved of immeasurable help.

Mr. and Mrs. Henry Christy, of Anselmo, showed me pictures and told me stories about the early towns of Custer County, especially Anselmo and Broken Bow.

The late Leigh DeLay, historian for the Nebraska State Historical Society, answered questions and directed me in some of my research. John E. Carter, Curator of Photographs of the Nebraska State Historical Society, dug up hundreds of pictures for me to search through and copied the ones that I needed.

There are many others to whom I owe my gratitude for their contributions. A project like this cannot be accomplished alone. I want to say thanks to all those, both listed and unlisted, who extended a helping hand.

Those Who Went Before

First the trapper and fur trader; then the gold seeker; and then the emigrant forged trails across what was to become Nebraska. But for their trailblazing, exploration, and claiming land from the native Americans, there would have been no place for the town builder.

The Indians resented this invasion of their homeland and hunting grounds, and struck back. To easterners, nestled snugly in cities far to the morning side of the Mississippi, the country west of the Missouri was an untamable wilderness. The Indians, in their efforts to stem the tide of white invaders, put the stamp of conviction on the easterners' opinion.

Every type of draft animal was used in the migration to Oregon, Utah, and, especially, California after the discovery of gold there. One of the most durable, but also the most obstinate, was the mule. One man, reporting on another's attempt to break a mule to the saddle, said that he was thrown, "hell, west and crooked."

Fort Kearny moved from the Missouri to the Platte river in 1848. All the trails along the Missouri, from Independence and Westport Landing north to Council Bluffs, converged at Fort Kearny and followed the Platte west toward the mountains.

No one could foresee the flood of people who would pass by in the years just ahead. Before long, a cluster of sod buildings sprang up just to the west of Fort Kearny, off the military reservation. It was officially named Kearney City but everyone called it Doby-town. It was as wild as a prairie town of the '50s and '60s could be and gave a brief but distorted glimpse of the Kearney to come. It had a general and a dry goods store, a blacksmith shop, and a bevy of saloons.

People of every nationality swept across the Plains. As one man wrote, describing Dobytown and one of the saloons where he had spent some time, "They spoke four languages there, English, Mexican, French and profanity."

Long novels have been written about murders on the trail, the trials that followed, and the punishment meted out. Merrill Mattes in his book, *The Great Platte River Road,* shows how briefly such a tale could be told. He quotes a traveler on the road up the Platte who reported: "Young shot Scott dead. The company had a trial and found him guilty. They gave him a choice to be hung or shot. He preferred being shot, and was forthwith." On the trail, they had little time for the niceties or ceremonies of the city courtroom.

Cholera, not murder, was the great killer. In the 1850s, the route from the Little Blue river to Fort Laramie resembled an unorganized cemetery. Travelers over the trail in 1850 estimated one thousand graves between the Little Blue and Scott's Bluff. Others put the estimate as high as five thousand. Yet relatively few emigrants gave up and returned. They were made of tough fiber.

This toughness, stubbornness, courage—whatever—also dominated the lives of those who eventually settled on the Nebraska rivers, hills and prairies. Without it, Nebraska never would have been transformed from the prairie home of Indians and buffalo to the breadbasket of today that feeds many times the population of the state.

In 1854, Nebraska Territory was created and the Indians were pushed farther from the Missouri. Omaha, Nebraska City, Brownville, and a dozen other towns suddenly bloomed along the west bank of the river.

The displaced Indians struck back at the white men who crossed the territory in 1864 and 1865. The *Omaha Daily Nebraskan* reported some of the stories told by people arriving at Fort Kearny.

One man traveling to Denver came into Fort Kearny on the stage and described what he saw on his ride from Kiowa Station, approximately eighty miles to the southeast along the Little Blue River, close to present-day Hebron. He reported that two men had been killed by Indians at Kiowa Station. Seven miles farther to the northwest at Oak Grove Ranch, they found two more men murdered. Four miles farther on, they found another pair dead, stripped of all their clothing.

A short distance farther, at Eubanks' ranch, they came upon a young woman dead. She had been scalped and mutilated. Eubanks himself, his two sons and daughter were also dead. A small child of Eubanks' had been carried away by the Indians.

Farther along, close to Thirty-two Mile Creek, they discovered a six-wagon freight train that had been attacked. All the drivers were killed and the stock stolen. Goods were scattered everywhere. This was south of present-day Hastings, approximately where the trail left the Little Blue and headed for a junction with the trail from Nebraska City.

To the southwest of Kearny on Plum Creek, the Indians attacked a wagon train, killing all eleven men. The *Nebraska Advertiser* of Brownville, Nebraska, on August 18, 1864, reported on the Plum Creek Massacre:

The men killed at Plum Creek were first wounded and kept lying on the ground while the savages had a war dance around them. They were finally tortured to death and then scalped. Two women were taken into captivity from Plum Creek.

The raids finally tapered off and traffic cautiously resumed. Few travelers turned back. It had been a crucible from which the kind of men emerged who would build towns to anchor the wanderer and transform the wilderness into prosperous communities.

In 1867 the railroad pushed its ribbons of steel along a route paralleling the trail up the Platte River. The Indians could not fight the iron horse and dropped back to more remote areas, leaving the land to white settlers.

It would seem that the settlers would have suffered their fill of trouble and fighting by this time and an aura of peace would have fallen over the prairie. Perhaps it was the arrival of newer settlers who hadn't been drained by fear and exhaustion. Or maybe it was the ex-soldiers who had grown so accustomed to fighting that peace made them uncomfortable.

Whatever the reason, as the towns sprang up on the prairie, trouble often erupted and, despite the best efforts of residents, they earned reputations as wild towns.

WILD TOWNS OF NEBRASKA

Chapter 1

Omaha

It was once said that every baby boy born in the United States was a potential future president. Likewise, every town born on the Nebraska plains in the 1850s and 1860s was a potential state capital.

Many towns sprang up along the Missouri River during the spring and summer of 1854. All suffered birth pains, and many were stillborn. But not Omaha—it was a husky, kicking, squalling infant from the moment of its first cry.

Until 1854, Nebraska was Indian territory. White men were not legally permitted to settle there. Then came the bill introduced into Congress by Stephen A. Douglas proposing the Territory of Nebraska. In Douglas' words, it was, "to serve notice on the Secretary of War to discontinue using that territory as a dumping ground for Indians."

The bill was defeated in 1851 and again in 1853 but on May 30, 1854, the Kansas-Nebraska Bill passed and became law. The land west of the Missouri River was open to white settlement.

Still, the emigrants pouring across the river faced another legal problem: the land was not surveyed and since it was still federal land, only the federal government could issue a deed to any of it.

Those early pioneers were not slowed by a little item such as that. They counted on the preemption law of 1841, allowing a man to preempt a parcel of land and, after establishing residency, bid it in for a reasonable price at an auction. So they immediately began preempting the land they wanted.

However, 160 acres was all that a man could preempt. The early arrivals decided to raise it to 320 acres per man. The fact that this was illegal was of no concern. They were here first—they'd make their own laws.

They formed what they called a Claim Club. Each man would take 320 acres and any "claim jumper" would be removed, either politely or forcibly. When the Territorial Legislature was established, Claim Club members got this law put on the books. In their eyes, this made it absolutely legal. They ignored the fact that only the federal government could give legal title to the land.

The Preemption Law of 1841 stated that a man who took preemptory rights to a quarter had to put up a building within thirty days or lose his right to claim the land. When a man found a quarter with no house, he could reasonably assume it was unclaimed.

This was not the case in Omaha. To avoid conflicts, the Claim Club made a rule that every new man coming into the district must get permission from the club before taking any land. This rule was challenged by George "Doc" Smith, veteran surveyor of Douglas County. Finding an unoccupied quarter with no building, he claimed it and began constructing a house. After only a few days and half his house built nearly a hundred men appeared, marching toward him. They were well armed. Smith decided his smartest move was to disappear. He backed off to a small clump of trees and hid, watching the men tear down his house and burn the lumber.

George "Doc" Smith

The *Omaha Daily Nebraskan* reported a humorous version of an incident that occurred in July 1857. An Irishman named Dennis Dee had squatted on some unclaimed land in Irishtown—also referred to as Gophertown because there were so many dugouts there. However, he had not secured permission from the Claim Club to settle there. Enforcers of the club, sometimes called vigilantes, sometimes regulators, were given the task of punishing Dennis Dee for his flagrant disregard of their club's rules.

The regulators went to Irishtown in force and stormed into the house that Dee had built. But they'd made a slight miscalculation; the man of the house was not home. The women and children of Irishtown were duly frightened but the regulators had no quarrel with them.

Neighbors quickly relayed word to the oth-er men of Irishtown wherever they happened to be working. The men rushed home, armed themselves with guns and shillalahs, and drove the regulators out of town. The regulators felt that the battle was lost but not the war. That evening they returned in stronger force. Irishtown residents, however, inspired by their earlier victory, were expecting a renewal of the fight and were ready with better arms and a larger army. Again they put the vigilantes to flight and in the words of the *Omaha Daily Nebraskan* reporter:

The wanderers from Florence* suddenly recollected that they had some business to transact at their homes and they turned and fled towards Florence—running with the speed of the wind towards home and with the tails of their coats sticking straight out behind them, and the bullets which followed them were not swift enough to catch them.

To this day, all that is necessary to arouse the anger of a man from Florence is to mention the fourth letter of the alphabet.

It wasn't often that a squatter won against the Claim Club. With a gang of over a hundred armed men, the vigilantes would move against anyone who had claimed land without the consent of the club.

One of these unfortunates was Jacob Shull. He had built on unoccupied land but when he saw the armed mob coming his way, he knew what they were after and took the only sane course—he hid.

The mob tore down his buildings and set fire to the lumber. Then they began searching for him. Guessing his life was in danger, Schull took refuge in a dry goods store for two days.

Mormon Ox Cart, 14th and Douglas Streets, 1860

*Florence at that time was a few miles north of Omaha. The site of Florence is now a residential section of Omaha.

But the strain of hiding and losing everything he had bore heavily on Jacob Shull. Within a year he died. His death as a fairly young man was attributed by most to the treatment he had received at the hands of the Claim Club.

After disposing of Jacob Shull, the Claim Club turned its attention to an Irishman named Callahan who had settled on open land claimed by a member of the club. They ran Callahan off the land but in a few days he returned. So the vigilantes arrested him and brought him in for trial by the club. He was quickly found guilty and given the choice of renouncing his claim or being drowned in the Missouri River.

Callahan was stubborn and refused to give up his land. The vigilantes took him to the river, cut a hole in the ice, and dropped him in. One man held on to him because the current would have swept him under the ice if he had let go.

They dragged him out on the ice and demanded he sign over his claim. When he refused, he was ducked a second time. After a third time, he was dragged out, so weak he couldn't stand. Callahan realized that if he didn't give up his claim, they'd let go of him the next time they ducked him—he'd be found in the spring somewhere far down the river.

After he agreed to sign over his claim, the vigilantes took Callahan back to the building where he had been tried but he was too weak to stand or hold a pen. They stripped his frozen clothes and warmed him up enough to sign the papers before he was released. He never regained his health and died a few years later.

Another Irishman showed his stubborn streak a short time later when he was arrested for claiming land a club member said was his. When ordered to release his claim, he refused. He was tied up, thrown into a wagon, and the wagon driven under a huge cottonwood. A rope was thrown over a limb of

the tree and the noose put around his neck. Still the Irishman refused to give up his claim. He was pulled up on the rope and left long enough to strangle the breath from him, and then dropped down. When he was recovered enough to talk, he hadn't changed his mind. He was jerked off the wagon bed again. This time his suspension was longer before he was let down.

Stubbornness was this man's middle name and still he refused to relinquish his claim. The mob made a choice. Hang him until he was dead or try a different method. They chose to starve him. They locked up him and stood guard over him. After a few days, the torture of starvation got to the Irishman and he agreed to sign over his land. He was released with the admonition never to show up again.

One of the first—probably the very first— murder cases in Omaha erupted in April 1855. It actually took place in Bellevue but it was the Omaha officials who had to take charge of the investigation.

A doctor by the name of Charles Henry had shot a man named George Hollister. The argument had been over the boundary line between two town lots. Henry was a speculator in town lots as well as a doctor. Four men from Omaha, including Sheriff Peterson, made the trip to Bellevue, arriving there about midnight. They found Henry a prisoner in the blacksmith shop, guarded from men who threatened to lynch him.

Henry insisted that he had killed Hollister in self-defense but others disagreed. Henry was brought up before Judge Ferguson for examination, but because the evidence was not conclusive, the judge ordered him held for a full jury trial. Since there was no jail, the judge decreed that he be kept in the sheriff's house, feet shackled, handcuffed, and chained to the floor.

How the trial would have come out if it had been held then will never be known. Circumstances worked in favor of the doctor. Cholera had broken out among a detach-

Courtesy Nebraska State Historical Society
Judge Fenner Ferguson

ment of soldiers coming up the river by boat. They asked for a doctor and Dr. Miller, who treated the sick in town, was taken upriver with the soldiers. That left only Dr. Henry, so he was taken around the town still in shackles by the sheriff, to administer to the sick. He made many friends as he went the rounds and when the jury was finally impaneled, there were many former patients ready to testify to Dr. Henry's good character so he was set free. Dr. Henry stayed on in Omaha to become a prominent citizen and greatly helped the Union cause during the Civil War.

Two men, who obviously felt that thievery was an easier way to make a living than working, stole two horses in Omaha. As well as being thieves, the men were lazy. Instead of taking the horses far away to dispose of them, they sold them to some Pawnee Indians at Elkhorn, only a short distance from Omaha. The horses got away from the Indians and wandered back home.

When the Indians came into Omaha on the trail of the horses and declared their ownership, the original owners disputed and explained that the Indians had bought stolen property. The next time white men tried to sell them horses, they informed the Indians, they should arrest them and bring them into Omaha where they could prove whether or not they were the rightful owners of the animals they were trying to sell.

It happened that the next white men who tried to sell some animals to the Indians were the same men who had sold them the horses. Remembering the horses they had bought and lost before, the Indians followed instructions, taking the two men into custody and transporting them to Omaha.

Since there was no law to punish the men, the settlers who had been plagued by horse and cattle thieves decided to do it themselves. Their trial was swift and the sentence sure. They must return to the Indians the money they had received for the stolen horses. Then they would have their heads shaved and be given thirty-nine lashes on their bare backs.

The Negro barber shaved only half of the hair on each head. After some debate as to who would administer the lashes, the owners of the horses were given the task. The flogging took place on a vacant block bounded by today's Farnam, Harney, 12th and 13th Streets. The Indians enjoyed the spectacle much more than those who had decreed it. Still, the settlers felt it was necessary if they were to stop the stealing.

As soon as the whippings were over, the thieves were taken to the river and told to leave. They were not seen near Omaha again.

That did not stop the horse stealing, however. In March of 1858, after law and order had supposedly come to Omaha, another case of horse stealing was handled by the Claim Club.

This time, the horses were stolen from men near Florence. The vigilantes took to the trail with the determination of bloodhounds.

They caught up with the two thieves, Braden and Daley, brought them back, and had them put in jail to await trial.

The courthouse was only partially finished but the jail was complete, as was the sheriff's office. Cam Reeves was the sheriff at this time. That evening, Reeves left the office for some reason while his wife kept watch. There seemed little to worry about.

But while the sheriff was gone one man walked boldly into the office and took the key to the jail cell. Others hurried in and the two prisoners were dragged out of the jail before the sheriff's wife could sound the alarm.

The thieves were thrown into a wagon, hands and feet bound, and the wagon headed north out of town at a fast clip. The commotion had attracted the attention of several people who mounted horses and hitched up wagons and buggies and followed to see what would happen.

They went through Florence and came to a huge oak tree north of town. Using one rope, they tied a loop at each end, threw the rope over a stout limb, and put a loop around each man's neck. Then they drove the wagon out from under them.

The mob scattered after the hanging like a flock of frightened blackbirds. But repercussions set in quickly. The citizens of Omaha lived by law and order; they wanted vigilante justice stopped. The fact that the sheriff brought the bodies back the next day and put them in the same cell from which they had been taken the day before, and that rats chewed on the bodies during the night did nothing to lessen the demand that something be done about the way things were being handled.

An inquest was held with several reluctant witnesses who swore they could not identify any of the vigilantes involved. The law could do nothing. The sheriff was later convicted of dereliction of duty and issued a heavy fine.

The Claim Club quietly slipped into oblivion in 1857 and 1858 after the government surveyed the land and settled accounts with the squatters, allowing each man 160 acres. The idea of vigilance committees did not die with the Claim Club regulators, however, but now there was a difference. The new vigilantes were mostly decent citizens who were determined to see wrongs righted and wrongdoers punished, something the law often failed to do.

Their work began shortly after the Claim Club vigilantes disbanded. Gamblers were a big problem and the men of town felt they should be moved on. They sent a delegation, with masked faces and drawn guns, to call on each undesirable man and hand him a letter that gave him twenty-four hours to leave town. The message was usually delivered after midnight when they had to wake the man in order to make the delivery. The suggestion of leaving was never ignored. Sometimes they simply painted a skull and crossbones on the door where the man was sleeping. That was equally effective.

The following year, 1859, the vigilantes were given jurisdiction over the case of a young man caught burglarizing a jewelry store. The trial was short. It was in the dead of winter and the man was taken out to the bluff overlooking the Missouri. There they told him they were going to hang him. The man begged for his life.

They proceeded to hang him and then suddenly cut the rope, allowing him to fall into a deep snow drift. When he clawed his way out of that, the vigilantes began shooting at his feet. He plunged down the bluff and out on the ice of the river. The last they saw of him, he was making a raceway on the ice toward Council Bluffs.

The vigilantes got into a case in the spring of 1861 in which they had not planned to take a hand. Two men, apparent vagabonds, came to the house of George Taylor, northwest of Omaha. Their original purpose is guesswork. But they found George gone and his wife there alone.

The men, named Bouve and Iler, might have decided on the spur of the moment to rob the place since the man of the house was gone. They certainly hadn't planned on a spunky woman resisting as Mrs. Taylor did. Bouve got rough with her, tied her up and threw her on the bed. Then he demanded that she tell him where the money and valuables were kept in the house. She refused. Bouve hit her and threatened to set the bed on fire. Iler objected to that; he only wanted to rob the place.

They left Mrs. Taylor bound on the bed while they ransacked the house, taking what money they could find and throwing the silverware and any other valuables into a pillowcase.

Bouve was sure they had not found the real cache of money so he went back to Mrs. Taylor and threatened her again. This time he pointed a gun at her head but once more Iler stopped him. He wasn't going to be involved in murder. Bouve put the gun away and they left with what they had. They went into Omaha and buried the sack full of money and valuables near an old brickyard close to the river.

When George Taylor got home he found his wife bound on the bed and his house ransacked. He first set things straight and then went into Omaha and reported the theft. Mayor Armstrong, who was also police judge of Omaha, swore out a warrant for the two men and gave it to the city marshal. Not knowing the names of the two thieves, Marshal Riley had little to go on.

Later that day, he observed two unfamiliar men playing cards in a saloon. They seemed overly free with money for not appearing to be wealthy men. He arrested them on suspicion and took them before Judge Armstrong. They gave their names as James Bouve and John Iler. The judge had them searched but they had only a little money and nothing that would tie them to the robbery of the Taylor house. So they were released with apologies, but after they were gone the judge ordered Riley to keep a close watch on them.

Then the judge sent word to George Taylor to bring his wife into town the next morn-

Omaha — Looking east on Farnam, 1860

ing and told Riley to arrest the pair again at that time. Marshal Riley followed the two men back to the saloon beneath the Western Exchange building. Bouve and Iler were bragging that they would set the town on fire because they had plenty of money coming from friends in a day or two.

Marshal Riley arrested them the next morning down by the river. It appeared that they might be preparing to leave town and Riley was determined to take them to the judge before they got away. Bouve and Iler weren't far from the spot where they had buried the sack the day before but Riley did not know that.

The Taylors had reached town. The judge put Mrs. Taylor in a back room where no one would see her. Spectators were crowding the courtroom because they had seen the marshal bring in the two vagabonds.

The judge lined spectators up along the walls, placing Bouve and Iler among them. He called in Mrs. Taylor and asked her whether she could identify the two robbers if she saw them again. She made it very clear that she could pick them out of a thousand people.

She walked slowly down the line until she came to Bouve. She stopped dead still and glared at him. "You are the man who wanted to kill me!" she shouted.

A little farther down the line, she stopped in front of Iler. "You are the man who saved my life. You said, 'Don't shoot that old woman.'"

The judge put both men in jail in separate cells. After a short time, the marshal went to Bouve and told him that Iler had confessed. But Bouve wouldn't crack. So he went to Iler's cell and told him that Bouve had confessed. Iler crumbled and told everything about the robbery, including where they had buried the loot. Marshal Riley took Iler down to the river near the brickyard and recovered the sack of valuables taken from the Taylor home. Then he put Iler back in jail.

The next day a large crowd of men met without the marshal's knowledge to talk over the details of the robbery. They decided to hold a trial immediately for the two men. The law would take a long time and Bouve and Iler might escape justice. So twelve men were chosen for the jury and lawyers were selected for both sides. The defense lawyers insisted that the two prisoners were entitled to a trial in the courts. The other lawyers repeated what Mrs. Taylor said had happened. The jury decided that the vigilantes should dispose of the case.

What the vigilantes would do was a foregone conclusion. Nothing was said or done to change that. At midnight a mob of masked men moved into the courthouse. They overpowered Marshal Riley who was guarding the jail, passing him out over the heads of the men like a sack of flour. Then they found the keys to the cells.

Courtesy Nebraska State Historical Society
Omaha City in 1865

Thirteenth and Farnam Streets,
looking northwest, 1863.

They unlocked Bouve's cell and looked for a place to hang him. All the men were masked heavily so each could truthfully say he hadn't seen the faces of any of the vigilantes. In spite of the grimness of the moment, they got a laugh when one man, whose voice was identifiable to any who knew him, squeaked out that he had found a beam from which they could hang Bouve.

This they promptly did, but they took Iler outside the jail and told him to leave town, firing shots after him as he ran. His stand in keeping Mrs. Taylor alive had saved him from hanging beside his partner.

On Valentine's Day, Friday, 1868, Otway G. Baker was hanged in Omaha for the murder of Woolsey D. Higgins. It had taken two trials and the denial of a third to make his conviction stand. Many would have gone on believing in his innocence had he not written a complete confession just before the hour of his execution.

On November 23, 1866, Otway Baker culminated a plan to rob the store where he worked. From his confession, it is obvious that he had planned it carefully. On this night he had gone to bed early. When

Woolsey Higgins came to bed later, he had gone to him, demanding money. Higgins refused and Baker realized that the only way he could make his plan work was to murder Higgins.

After killing Higgins, he went to the safe, got the money, quickly took it outside and hid it. Then he came back into the building, took off his outer clothes again and set fire to the store, starting it in the cellar with coal oil and old boards. His intention was for the fire to burn through the floor so that the heavy weight of the goods would crash down and crush the body of Higgins. Then no one would be able to tell how he had been killed.

Baker fired a shot in his own arm so that he would appear to have been wounded in the robbery. After shooting himself, he threw the gun into the fire and ran out into the street, yelling, "Fire! Murder!"

A man ran to the fire station and rang the bell. Baker ran back and forth in a good imitation of a man beside himself with fright and grief.

When the fire engine arrived and started spraying, the water knocked a box of matches off a shelf and scattered them over the

Taken in 1871, this view shows the Union Pacific depot at approximately the location where it is today.

bed. This made authorities, examining the building after the fire was out, suspect that the fire had been deliberately set and point a suspicious finger at Baker. The matches had nothing to do with the fire but the suspicion was planted and persisted into the trials.

Baker's attorneys, who had believed Baker was innocent until he made his confession, insisted on a poll of each of the jurors at the second trial. Each said he was convinced that Baker was guilty. The lawyers asked for a new trial on a couple of techni-

calities. When that was denied, Baker was sentenced to be hanged. That sentence was carried out on February 14, 1868, shortly after Baker had written his confession.

Like most frontier towns, Omaha had a rather wild beginning; this has been just a glimpse. It took some effort to trim away the rough edges of its history but when the trimming was done, there was a solid foundation on which was built the largest city in Nebraska.

Sheeley Town Station in Omaha, circa 1900

Chapter 2

Nebraska City

The settlement that was to become Nebraska City was begun while Nebraska was still Indian territory. Riverboats on the Missouri put in here and disgorged westbound travelers with their wagons and teams. Other emigrants crossed here from southwest Iowa.

In 1846 Colonel Stephen Watts Kearny was sent to set up a new fort near the confluence of Table Creek and the Missouri River, on the west side of the big river. They named it Fort Kearny. Before much of the fort had been built, the army realized that most of the traffic was coming from Independence and St. Joseph, Missouri, and hitting the Platte River in Nebraska west of its big northern loop.

Admitting their error in location, the military moved the fort west to the Platte River, close to the spot where the trails from Council Bluffs and Independence met. Here, in 1848, they established what became the permanent Fort Kearny.

The gold rush of 1849 and 1850 increased the traffic immensely all along the Missouri River. The crossing at the abandoned Old Fort Kearny was no exception. The eastern half of the Oregon Trail became the California Trail too.

In 1854 Nebraska City was platted around the site of Old Fort Kearny. One traveler said the old blockhouse was right on Main Street, near the center of the new town.

April 23, 1856, was the date of the first murder in Nebraska City. It exploded from a quarrel over a claim. Benjamin Lacey was the victim, Simpson Hargus the survivor. There was no doubt about the guilt of Hargus. But a member of the territorial legislature from Nebraska City, A. A. Bradford, took the defense of Hargus. He managed to stall the trial until he was able to get a bill through the legislature repealing the entire criminal code of the territory. That left no grounds on which to prosecute Hargus and he was set free.

In 1859, Nebraska City had an influx of gold seekers, this time heading for Colorado. That year also brought local troubles.

Courtesy Nebraska State Historical Society

Block House at Old Fort Kearny. It was built between 1846 and 1847 and then torn down in 1889.

NEW ADVERTISEMENTS.

ARMY OF THE WEST!

16,000 YOKE
OF
GOOD WORKING CATTLE,

From Four to 7 years of age, wanted at

NEBRASKA CITY,

for hauling freight from this point to Utah, for which SEVENTY-FIVE DOLLARS per Yoke will be paid. Notice will be given through the newspapers of the time they are to be delivered, but suppose they will be wanted about the first of May.

FIFTEEN HUNDRED MEN

Wanted for teamsters who will be found and paid Twenty-five dollars per month out and back.

None but men of good habits need apply; as drinking intoxicating liquors, card playing; and profane language will not be permitted while in employment. Each man will be presented with a Bible and hymn book. Forty Wagon Masters wanted who must come well recommended and who will be paid the usual wages.

A number of houses will be rented in Nebraska City, and one large store room. Apply to
RUSSELL, MAJORS & WADDEL.
by KINNEY & HOLLY, Agents.   Mr 20-1

Courtesy Nebraska State Historical Society
"Army of the West" Advertisement, March 1857

The motivation for one murder seems to have been nothing but revenge. On Saturday, June 4, 1859, a man named Charless, a leading citizen of St. Louis, was in Nebraska City when a man named Thornton gunned him down in the street in broad daylight. The only excuse for such an act seemed to be that in years past, Charless had testified at Thornton's trial and his testimony helped to convict Thornton of embezzling money from the Boatman's Savings Institution. Thornton had been secretary of the institution at the time.

Charless was well liked, and within an hour citizens of the town were up in arms, ready for a lynching party. It took some persuasion to prevent the mob from dealing out the justice they deemed warranted. Law and order prevailed and Thornton was held for a legal trial, the outcome of which seems to be lost to history.

Less than three weeks after the murder of Charless, on the 22nd of June, another incident occurred that some citizens felt called for lynch law. These were witnesses who could testify that a man named Simpson tried to stop James Marshall while he was driving his buggy along the levee. He grabbed the bridle of one of the horses and stopped the team. Marshall stood up and yelled for Simpson to let go of his team.

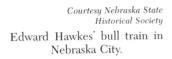

Courtesy Nebraska State Historical Society
Edward Hawkes' bull train in Nebraska City.

Simpson reached into his pocket, pulled out a large revolver and fired at Marshall. The bullet hit Marshall under the chin and went through his neck. When Marshall toppled over, Simpson left the scene.

Constable Hulin was notified and he arrested Simpson. Simpson seemed to think it was all a joke. But as Hulin marched him along the levee, Simpson asked whether he really was arresting him. Hulin assured him that he was. Hulin had made the error of not searching Simpson for his gun. Now Simpson pulled his gun and leveled it at the constable.

A man named G. M. Hail was standing a few feet away. Seeing danger threatening the constable, he leaped between the two men as Simpson fired. Somehow the bullet went between them and neither one was hit. They overpowered Simpson and he was taken away to the blockhouse to await trial, again avoiding a lynching but not several years in prison.

Despite efforts by the law and the vigilantes horse stealing was more the rule than the exception in the late 1850s and through the 1860s near Nebraska City. But the citizen arrest of S. O. Arnold by two men south of Nebraska City shocked the town.

Arnold came from a good family and was a graduate of Michigan University, a goal few men achieved in those days. He lived in Nebraska City and owned considerable property. To have him accused of stealing horses, arrested, and taken to Brownville was more than some could fathom.

Arnold was suspected of stealing a horse and a yoke of oxen. The authorities confined him to a room in the Brownville House, pending a hearing the next day before a justice of the peace.

Clayton, one of Arnold's accusers, had found a horse that had been stolen from him. The man keeping the horse said that Arnold had left it in his care.

Arnold apparently was not aware that Clayton had found his horse when he came to Clayton's place to spend the night. There was nothing unusual about a man of Arnold's stature spending the night with an honest farmer like Clayton. But the next morning, Clayton and a neighbor, George Simpson, arrested Arnold and took him to Brownville.

Arnold saw that his problems were catching up with him. Once in the Brownville House, he wrote a long letter to his wife in Nebraska City, giving her instructions about how to handle his financial affairs and declaring his innocence of any crime.

Then he tried to commit suicide but was caught and stopped. Before going to dinner, the guard made sure that Arnold had nothing on him with which to kill himself, since his first attempt had proven he was inclined to do just that.

When the guard returned from dinner, however, he found that Arnold had outsmarted him. With a strap less than three feet long, he had managed to hang himself. Fastening one end of the strap to the bed rail, he had buckled the other end around his neck and stretched out, his head only inches from the floor, his hands free. He had choked himself to death.

Within an hour of discovering Arnold's suicide, the Brownville sheriff was visited by the sheriff of Otoe County. He had a warrant for Arnold's arrest for stealing horses near Nebraska City. The sheriff said there was a waiting list of people between Brownville and Nebraska City wanting to take Arnold from the authorities and lynch him.

In May 1860, a devastating fire swept through Nebraska City, destroying almost all the city north of Table Creek. But the town quickly recovered, survived the Civil War in the middle of a battle zone where the North and South lapped against each other, and emerged with a mixed bag of transients that kept the town on edge.

One man who visited Nebraska City in 1866 described a first class hotel: "With a few exceptions the crowds of men who thronged the dining hall at mealtimes were armed with pistols. There was one pecu-

Courtesy Nebraska State Historical Society

Central Avenue, Nebraska, City, 1866.

liarity—not one man in ten would look me squarely in the face. Those who would not meet the eye, I set down as, 'Rebs,' 'deserters,' 'bushwhackers,' or 'guerillas,' and there are any amount of them there. This winter it has not been safe for a man to go on the streets after dark alone."

On August 15, 1866, a cowardly murder took place just five miles outside Nebraska City. It aroused the indignation of the public like few things cold because the victim was an eleven-year-old boy. The boy was William Henry Hamilton and he was doing what many boys his age did, herding his father's cattle so they could graze but not wander off on the fenceless prairie.

When the boy did not return home with the cattle toward evening, his father went in search of him. He found him in a creek close to where he had been herding. He had been shot three times, twice in the head and once in the body. The cattle were gone.

The body was taken home and word of the murder spread through the neighborhood. Anger and a cry for revenge rose. It took only a short time to identify the killer. A cattle buyer named Hayes in Nebraska city had bought some cattle that afternoon. A check of the cattle showed they were Hamilton's.

By that time nearly two hundred men were armed and feverish to take the trail. The man they were looking for had called himself Cash. There had been two men with him, Deitch and Ford. The unauthorized posse, more closely resembling a mob, wanted all three men.

They located Deitch and Ford but Cash, who they were sure had done the killing, had fled across the Missouri river into Iowa. A small group of determined men from the mob crossed the river too. Their authority was just as potent in Iowa as it was in Nebraska since it was not considered legal law enforcement anywhere.

At a place called Plum Hollow in southwest Iowa, they captured their man the next morning. They discovered that his real name was Casper Frederick Diercks. They suppressed the urge to hang him on the spot and brought him back to Nebraska City. Most of the people in town lined the banks of the Missouri River as the captive was returned to the Nebraska side.

The impatience of the crowd to see justice done would not allow for a formal trial. At ten thirty that morning, court was set up in an open square in town. A president, D. J. McCann, was named and another man,

Dan Lauer, was made secretary to record the proceedings. In spite of some speeches admonishing restraint, a jury of citizens was selected and the trial began.

The dead boy's father was called as a witness. So was the cattle buyer, and the two men arrested as Diercks' accomplices, Sebastian Deitch and R. P. Ford. There was little doubt in the minds of the observers that Diercks was the murderer. He was the mastermind of the plot and he was the one who had sold the cattle and taken the money. Perhaps it was the testimony of his two accomplices that drove the final nails into his coffin.

For not having any legal authority, the men in control gave the trial all the legal appearance possible. After the jury found Diercks guilty of the brutal murder, he was sentenced to be hanged but the actual hanging was postponed until six o'clock that evening to give the condemned man time to prepare himself for his fate.

At six o'clock he was hanged in spite of his insistence that he was not guilty of murder. Few, if any, doubted his guilt. The two men who had been in Diercks' company, Deitch and Ford, were turned over to the real authorities to await trial for their part in the murder and theft.

Just before primary day in May 1867, a shooting overshadowed news of the coming election. On Thursday, May 9, Augustus Nelson was in town. Gus lived with Albert Tuxbury's family, about a mile and a half outside town, but he often stayed in town overnight. Albert Tuxbury had practically raised young Gus Nelson. Gus was getting an outfit together to take a train of freight wagons across the plains to Denver. Since his work was keeping him late, he decided to spend the night in town rather than return to Tuxbury's place.

He reserved a room at the Colorado House and went back to finish his business. Somewhere between eleven and twelve o'clock, he finished his work and walked back to the Colorado House. The door being locked, he knocked. A man named Jim Wishardt answered, calling through the door for identification of the visitor.

Nelson told him who he was and that he had reservations for a bed that night. Wishardt apparently was not convinced; he wouldn't open the door. The two argued for a minute and finally Nelson gave up and turned back up the street. He had friends in the city; he could stay with one of them.

He had gone only a few steps when the door behind him opened and Wishardt appeared with a gun in his hand. He fired three times, hitting Nelson once in the back close to the spine, and puncturing his lung.

Nelson went down, knowing he was seriously wounded. Seeing Wishardt still in the doorway, he called to him to get him to Dr. Larsh's office. Wishardt refused. He finally stepped back inside, shutting the door and locking it again.

No one responded to the shots and Nelson was left alone. Knowing he would die if he didn't get help, he dragged himself for a ways and finally staggered to his feet and wobbled down the street toward the doctor's office. He wouldn't have made it, though, if he hadn't been found by a man who helped him to the office and got the doctor.

Jim Wishardt was arrested and held in jail,

Courtesy Nebraska State Historical Society

Bull of the Woods Freighting Train leaving Nebraska City for Denver in the early 1860s.

waiting to see whether Gus Nelson lived or died. Dr. Larsh did the best he could for him but gave little hope for his recovery.

Fortunately, his diagnosis was wrong. Nelson was young and strong and he slowly recovered, taking six weeks to get back on his feet.

There is no record of what happened to Jim Wishardt so far as punishment for the shooting was concerned. He was still in Nebraska City that fall, a free man, because he registered as a voter in the general election.

Even as late as 1869, the law of the rope was occasionally used to assure swift and permanent justice. That year, on Saturday, November 13 while the ferryboat was crossing the river, a man named Charles Murphy fired several shots at the passengers on the ferry. One bullet hit the fireman, Dick Johnson, in the jaw, coming out near his ear.

It wasn't long afterward that someone found the body of Charles Murphy swinging from a tree near the ferry landing. It stayed there until the coroner cut it down. The men with the rope didn't even wait to find out whether Dick Johnson lived or died to mete out justice they felt was deserved.

One of the more bizarre incidents in Nebraska City happened after it seemed that law and order should have been in control. It ended on July 10, 1876, but its beginning was far to the west near the Colorado border in late September or early October, 1874.

James McGuire came from Otoe County, near Palmyra, west of Nebraska City. He hunted buffalo for their hides, most of which he sold in Wallace, Kansas. His hunting, however, was largely done in southwestern Nebraska.

McGuire had sold his hides in Wallace, Kansas, probably to Peter Robidoux, and received over fifteen hundred dollars for them. Outfitting for another hunt, he headed north. Two other hunters, Henry Dodge and Walter Hardin, followed him. They had done some bragging about going after a man up north but those boasts were forgotten until after the two were arrested.

Hank Dodge was about twenty years old; Walter Hardin was at least ten years older. They found McGuire camped along Frenchman Creek only a few miles east of the Colorado border in what would one day be Chase County, Nebraska. The details of that meeting were never revealed but the results were soon well known. The two men killed McGuire and threw his body into the slough running into the creek only a short distance away. They weighted the body down so it would not rise to the surface of the water. Then they took McGuire's team and wagon, which was probably the start of their downfall. If McGuire had any money left, and he surely had quite a bit, they took that, too.

They were then spotted in Julesburg, Colorado, approximately forty-five miles to the northwest, driving McGuire's team. The team was a distinctive one that many people of the area recognized. It was assumed that Dodge and Hardin had made a trade with McGuire.

Then another hunter, Asbury Buckmaster, happened along the Frenchman. When he passed the slough, he saw a man's boot sticking out of the water among the reeds. On closer examination, he discovered that a body was attached. The weight put on one leg had come off, allowing it to rise to the top of the shallow water.

Buckmaster pulled the body from the water, and found a letter in the man's pocket. Although water-soaked, it identified him as James McGuire. He buried the body close by. Buckmaster took the letter to Julesburg and mailed it to the *Omaha Bee* so that relatives of McGuire would know what happened to James and where he was buried. Then people recalled seeing Dodge and Hardin driving McGuire's team. While they weren't convinced that the two had killed McGuire, they did suspect they might have stolen the team and wagon. Dodge was a pleasant appearing young man and everyone seemed to like him. People felt that he had probably just appropriated a wandering team and wagon with no owner.

From Julesburg, Dodge and Hardin had gone south to Wallace, Kansas, where McGuire had outfitted before his trip to Nebraska. They drove the team through the town, bragging about getting the good rig from McGuire. After they had gone on, the men of Wallace decided McGuire wouldn't have sold that team. Dodge and Hardin must have stolen it.

A group of men went after the two and caught up with them at Granada, Colorado Territory, along the Arkansas River. They were taken to Hays, Kansas, and put in the Ellis County jail.

In the meantime, Peter McGuire, one of James McGuire's brothers, had read Buckmaster's letter in the *Omaha Bee* and the story of Buckmaster's finding McGuire's body in the slough on Frenchman Creek. He made a trip to Julesburg where he learned that two men were in jail in Hays, charged with stealing the team, wagon and gun of James McGuire. There was no mention of murder.

It took Peter McGuire some time to get the right papers to bring the murderers back to Nebraska. When he did, he had to bring them to the county seat of the area where the murder was committed. That was Stockville, county seat of Frontier County. At that time, all the land west of Frontier County to the state line was considered part of Frontier County because neither area had enough people to qualify as a county. Eventually these two areas would become Hays and Chase counties, but they wouldn't have the required population for over ten more years.

Stockville, however, had only a few buildings—there was no courthouse or any way to conduct a trial. The county transferred jurisdiction of the case to Otoe County at Nebraska City. So Dodge and Hardin were taken to Nebraska City, charged with murder, and jailed there to await trial.

Otoe County was the home of the McGuires. James McGuire had brothers and other relatives there. Also, there was an Irish settlement around Palmyra who considered James one of their own. As the trial date approached for Dodge and Hardin, the two prisoners complained of the prejudiced people in the county but their appeal netted them nothing.

An attorney was appointed for the defense; He promptly got a postponement of the trial until September while he acquainted himself with the facts. Hank Dodge, who could turn on the charm when required, soon had a few people believing in his innocence. That following grew as time went on. Officials commented that a verdict of guilty would have been a simple matter when the murderers first arrived in Nebraska City but by September, it was doubtful that a jury in Otoe County would convict the pair.

Meanwhile, Dodge and Hardin, with some inside help from people Dodge had converted to his plea of innocence, plotted an escape. They broke out of jail on June 4 and headed for the Republican River. One other prisoner went with them but he couldn't keep pace and was recaptured. He revealed their escape plan. The authorities caught up with the two murderers on the Republican River, just over the Kansas border, and brought them back to Nebraska City.

The jail break should have turned away all of Dodge's former friends. But they apparently were so convinced that he was getting the dirty end of the stick that they were only sorry he hadn't succeeded in his escape attempt.

Hardin was a sour faced criminal, evidently with a sour disposition too. He received none of the sympathy that Dodge was cultivating among his visitors. As the trial date in September approached, Hardin was convinced by the prosecuting attorneys to turn state's evidence in exchange for a prison term rather than a short rope and a long drop. His testimony at the trial counteracted all the good will Dodge had created for himself in the months before.—The jury returned a verdict of guilty of first-degree murder in the case of Hank Dodge.

Hardin was sent to the penitentiary at Lincoln to begin serving his sentence of twenty-five years for second-degree murder. Dodge was taken back to jail to await his execution, set for January 14, 1876. There he resumed his wooing of public sympathy while his attorneys demanded a retrial, saying he had been tried in the wrong county and that he wasn't present at his sentencing. Newspapers reporting the trial described Dodge's reaction during the sentencing so it seems likely that he was present. Nevertheless, the courts declared that he must be brought back into court and resentenced. This postponed his January 14 execution. Dodge used this extra time to appeal for his life to sympathizers outside the prison walls.

A large group of people, mostly women who opposed capital punishment, sent petitions to the governor at Lincoln, asking for a commutation of the death sentence to life imprisonment. Governor Garber did not ac-

Silas Garber, Governor of Nebraska during Hank Dodge's Trial

cede to the request but neither did he flatly refuse it.

Dodge wasn't resentenced until April 5, 1876, when he was sentenced to be hanged on July 21 of that year. More petitions flooded Governor Garber's desk on behalf of the convicted murderer until finally the governor made a trip to Nebraska City to see the prisoner in person. He was totally noncommittal about what he would do when he returned to Lincoln.

The feeling spread through Nebraska City that the governor would change the sentence to life imprisonment. For Dodge's friends, it seemed like a great victory. But to those who felt that a life for a life was fair play, it suggested a travesty of justice.

Sometime after midnight, just eleven days before the scheduled execution, a band of masked men surprised the jailor at the door. Peter McGuire, James's brother, overpowered him, tying him up. Just how many were in the band was never ascertained, but some ran inside the jail, threw a gun on the guard there and then shot Dodge as he lay chained to his cot. He was hit three times, twice in the body and once in the head. The masked men then disappeared like a fog in warm sunshine.

Dr. Larsh, the same doctor who had tended Gus Nelson when he was shot, was the doctor called to care for Hank Dodge. Dr. Larsh gave no hope for Dodge's recovery and this time his diagnosis was correct. Four days after he was shot, on July 14, Dodge died.

Efforts were made to find the vigilantes but they failed. All agreed that the ending was what the law had decreed; it was just reached in a different way.

As the town struggled to become an orderly community, the shadow of the rope hung over any criminal who was unquestionably guilty of a serious crime. More than two years after Hank Dodge paid with his life for murdering James McGuire, the vigilantes righted another wrong in Nebraska City.

On the last night in November, 1878, the

View of Nebraska City from the
Upland.

Judge William Gaslin

home of Charles Slocumb on Sioux Street was burglarized. They took what money they could find and murdered Slocumb. Mrs. Slocumb had seen the burglars and she threw suspicion on three black men, Henry Jackson, William Givens and Henry Martin. By ten o'clock the next morning, the three men had been found and arrested.

Court was in session at the time with the famous judge, The Honorable William Gaslin, known all over eastern Nebraska, presiding. A special trial date for the three men was set for December 6, less than a week after the murder.

Examination proved that William Givens, one of the three suspects, was not guilty of the murder, although he had a hand in the burglary. He was given the opportunity to turn state's evidence in exchange for release from charges. He accepted it.

The evidence against the other two was clear and irrefutable. The jury quickly brought back a verdict of guilty of second-degree murder. The sentence was life imprisonment. Henry Martin was heard to say that he would rather get the gallows than life imprisonment.

There were many in the courtroom and throughout the town who thought that life imprisonment was too light a sentence for the brutal murder of a well-known and well-liked citizen of Nebraska City.

The two convicted men were put in jail with guards watching them. About 2:00 A.M., a large body of armed men, all masked, came to the front door of the jail and demanded entrance. Deputy Sheriff McCallum refused.

The men were prepared for such a reply. They had a large log that they used as a battering ram against the door of the jail. After breaking in, they overpowered the deputy and took the keys to the cells. They had Martin and Jackson out of the jail in a minute and began marching them down Eleventh Street. An estimated crowd of two hundred people followed.

Across Table Creek bridge, they turned west to a tree with an obliging limb extending at right angles to the trunk. There they hanged the two men. The next morning the bodies were cut down and buried. When the presiding judge was told what had happened, he merely said, "I expected it."

Nebraska City was not yet ready for the prim and slow grinding process of law and order.

Chapter 3

Kearney

When the railroad began creeping along the Platte River in 1866 and 1867, towns erupted across the prairie. Like rowdy children shouldering their way into a gathering of adults, they did things that raised the eyebrows of their elders in the East.

Deciding that Fort Kearny was no longer needed, the government abandoned it in 1871. Moses Sydenham, postmaster at the fort, moved his post office a couple of miles west to Kearney City, the place everyone called Dobytown. Across the river, Kearney Station was striving to become an important town. Then the Burlington and Missouri River Railroad arrived, joining tracks with the Union Pacific about five miles west of this ambitious town. A new town sprang up and was named Kearney Junction. The little town of Kearney Station, now called Buda, was left behind with its shattered dreams, and Dobytown, with no soldiers to support it, sank back into the prairie.

Moses Sydenham promoted a plan to move the national capital from Washington, D.C. to the ten square miles of the abandoned

Cozad, on the one-hundredth meridian, forty miles west of Kearney, 1866

Burlington and Missouri Surveying Party, working west from Kearney toward North Platte.

Fort Kearny military reservation but the plan fizzled.

These ten square miles of lush bottomland grass was a temptation no cattleman could resist. The land wasn't open to settlement but letting cattle graze the grass wasn't going to hurt it.

The seeds of trouble grew as lush as the grass on the abandoned land. Cowboys responsible for keeping the cattle on the government land let them wander into neighboring fields of corn and cane.

The farmers screamed and demanded payment from the cattlemen. The cattlemen ignored them. Tempers soon frayed.

By 1874, Kearney was waiting for the storm. The cowboys, reinforced by more drovers from Texas, became bolder in their destruction of crops. Their trips into Kearney became more violent. A stop at one of the saloons seemed to trigger an uncontrollable desire to shoot up the town.

As the cowboys rode through the town on one occasion, firing their pistols at random, a bullet went through the dress of a small girl. Shortly after that, they chose a post as a target to demonstrate their accuracy, ignoring the fact that a man was leaning against

Moses Sydenham, postmaster, at the site of the first post office at Fort Kearny.

that post. The man escaped serious harm but the townspeople were furious. They organized themselves into an armed regiment to help the city marshal put a stop to the wild shooting sprees.

They knew the main tormentors, all from Texas. One was a dangerous man named Bill Bland. Another was Shoenberg, a name his friends had corrupted into Junebug. The third was known only as Texas Spence.

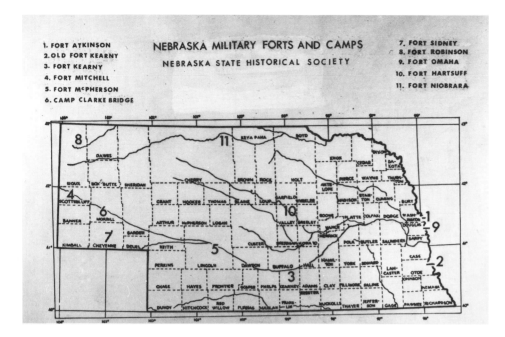

Nebraska Military Forts and
Camps.

The shooting began when Marshal Bricker attempted to quiet a fight that broke out. Bill Bland took a shot at the marshal and missed but the fuse was lit. Men flocked to the marshal's aid and before the shooting had ended, one cowboy named Peeler had been shot in the neck, although the wound did not prove fatal.

A few days later, another fight was triggered by Texas Spence when he fired a shot into a saloon. The streets suddenly filled with men carrying guns. Several shots were fired but nobody was injured.

Just two days after that, a well armed assault force of twenty-five or thirty herders rode into town, fortified their courage in a saloon, and then proceeded to Marshal Bricker's office.

Marshal Bricker was not there so the herders went to Weibel's Saloon. The men of Kearney now gathered and advanced on the saloon. There were about thirty armed men in the group, equaling the number of cowboys.

The herders were ordered out of town. Disorganized and already a little drunk, they retreated across the railroad tracks. But here their leaders rallied them. They had come to town looking for a confrontation; now they had it. Texas pride would not allow them to back off.

The cowboys started back toward the tracks. The Kearney townsmen were organized and ready for battle.

As the herders neared the railroad tracks, the town defenders fired some warning shots. The cowboys shot back and the battle was on. Shoenberg was wounded but stayed on his horse. Texas Spence was not so lucky. He took a bullet through the middle that almost paralyzed him. He fell from his horse in the path of the advancing townsmen. Although helpless, Spence tried to get his gun around to fire at the approaching men. One of the townsmen clubbed him over the head. The shot in the stomach would have killed Spence but the blow on his head hastened the end. The herders, seeing one of their leaders down and another wounded, retreated. The townsmen were happy to end the battle; if any of them were wounded, they didn't report it.

The cowboys withdrew to an island in the Platte River and camped, sending out threats that they would capture the town and burn it just as soon as they got reinforcements.

The townspeople could not risk taking the cowboys' threat lightly. Their defenders

23rd St. looking West, Kearney, Neb.

*Courtesy Nebraska State
Historical Society*
Looking west from 23rd Steet
in Kearney.

drilled each day close to the Burlington and Missouri River Railroad depot, which they used as their armory. Some favored storming the island and driving the herders away. Others preferred to wait, insisting the herders would soon leave after they realized they couldn't win.

In the meantime, Kearney posted a twenty-four hour guard at the edge of town to protect itself against surprise. The ones who advised patience won out. The cowboys did not try to burn the town.

Trouble with Texas herders broke out again a year later in September, 1875. A herd of sixty or seventy horses were the perpetrators. They were owned by Mayberry and Millet and had been brought up from Texas for sale to ranchers in the Nebraska sandhills.

While holding them south of town, the herders allowed them to get into Milton Collins' field. Collins took up about twenty-five horses to hold them until the owners paid for damages.

Collins rode into Kearney and obtained the necessary papers to force payment for damages. When he returned home, four of the herders came to get the horses. Jordon P. Smith served as their spokesman.

When told that Collins wanted pay for the damage the horses had done in his corn field, Smith swore and asked how much the damages would be. Collins told him that twenty dollars would cover it. Smith suddenly pulled his revolver and pointed it at Collins' head.

"If you say another word, I'll blow your brains out!" he yelled.

Then he ordered Collins to move on back toward the house. Collins obeyed the command, watching the gun pointed at his head. Every minute Smith dared Collins to say just one word. Collins apparently believed that Smith would shoot him if he so much as uttered a sound.

Near the house, Smith called a halt and ordered Collins to open the corral and let out the horses. But as Collins swung out of the saddle, Smith fired.

Collins hit the ground and ducked under the neck of his horse as Smith fired again. He fired three more times as Collins ran to the door of his house. Once inside the house, Collins fell, mortally wounded. Apparently the first shot had done the damage.

Two of the men with Smith, Joe Mitchell, from Missouri, and a Negro, Ben Mathews, from Texas, opened the corral gate and drove the horses back to the rest of the herd. Then the herders started the horses west up the Platte River valley.

Meanwhile, a doctor had been called but when he arrived, Milton Collins was dead. Collins' wife and father had witnessed the murder as had a couple of neighbors. Milton Collins was the son of Ashbury Collins, a former probate judge of Buffalo County; he was held in high esteem by everyone who knew him.

Within the hour word spread throughout Kearney that Collins had been murdered and his murderer was escaping up the river with a herd of horses. Men gathered quickly, armed with rifles and mounted on their best horses. They took up the pursuit.

They gained rapidly on the fleeing men. Smith, along with three other men, Ben Mathews and Joe Mitchell and a man called Yank, split from the herd and rode out into the hills. The men from Kearney divided into two groups. One group, under the leadership of Deputy U.S. Marshal D. B. Ball, followed the four, figuring the killer was among them. The other group, under Colonel John Roe, kept after the men still with the pony herd.

Deputy Marshal Ball's men got close enough to the four fleeing men to exchange shots with them but no one was hit. The four circled back and rejoined the rest of the men driving the horses. However, Colonel Roe and his men were so close to the herd that Smith and Yank left the herd again and tried to escape into the sandhills.

Colonel Roe caught up with the herd and demanded the surrender of the men. He expected a battle but they surrendered meekly. Ben Mathews and Joe Mitchell were among the prisoners taken back to Kearney.

It was about nine o'clock that night before Deputy Marshal Ball caught up with Jordon Smith and Yank on an island in the Platte River and forced them to surrender.

The preliminary hearing for Smith was held Monday morning in Kearney; he was indicted for murder. Twice he was convicted but his attorneys were able to get new trials for him. The third time, there was no appeal for a new trial and Smith was sentenced to ten years in the penitentiary.

As late as 1876, small raiding parties of Indians appeared in Buffalo County. One such party had been successful in stealing some fine horses. The problem was getting them back to the reservation through the thickly settled country.

Courtesy Nebraska State Historical Society
City Hall in Kearney

Courtesy Nebraska State Historical Society
Solomon D. Butcher Collection
Cowboy, foreman of the Watson ranch in Buffalo County, 1888

Before the raiding party had gone far, soldiers were on their trail. The pursuit was so pressing that the Indians had to let the stolen ponies go just to escape. They knew they could get away from the soldiers but they were furious at losing their horses.

It was this angry raiding party that struck three trappers along the South Loup River. A friend of the three men, John Marshall, was a teacher along Wood River. On this particular weekend he decided to visit his friends. The three men were living in a dugout with no windows. John saw nothing stirring when he arrived about ten o'clock so he pushed open the door. He found one of the men on the floor, shot in the chest and his head smashed with a heavy object.

It looked like the work of Indians. John cautiously went outside, scanning the surrounding hills for the culprits. The man inside had been killed very recently, perhaps within the hour. He began a search and found another of his friends just over the hill. He had also been shot and his face slashed with something, probably a tomahawk.

John didn't look for the third man. He was on foot and a long way from Kearney but it was the closest place to get help.

Knowing the ways of Indians, he tried to avoid brushy ravines where they might be camping. When he had to cross such a ravine, he approached it keeping a low profile, often crawling on his hands and knees. Making sure no one was within sight, he slipped into the ravine and up the opposite bank as quickly as possible.

He finally reached Wood River where he found a farm. Borrowing a horse, he rode on into Kearney and reported what he had found. A posse was quickly assembled. The

Courtesy Nebraska State Historical Society
U.S. Cavalry guarding overland mail, west of Fort Kearny.

posse found the bodies of the three men and shortly after that, less than a mile from the murder scene, the Indians. However, the posse was not able to catch the killers and they escaped to the reservation. There they melted into the Indian village, safely out of reach of the white man's law.

Perhaps the worst bad man who ever claimed Kearney as his temporary home was Samuel D. Richards. He had several other aliases. Few men left such a bizarre trail of vicious killings behind him.

Samuel Richards first appeared in the Kearney records in the summer of 1878 when he was arrested and jailed for stealing a watch. With him in jail was another man from south of the river named Harolsen (Harlston in some records), who was also in jail for theft. Harolsen and Richards became "friends."

Richards was due to be released first. He and Harolsen agreed that Richards would go to Harolsen's place and help Mrs. Harolsen take care of the homestead until her husband got out.

Released from jail, Richards went across the river to the Harolsen place. The Harolsens had four small children: Mary, Daisy, Mabel and Jessie, the baby. Shortly after Richards arrived at the Harolsen farm to take up the work, Mrs. Harolsen and her four children disappeared. Richards explained that she had become so discouraged while her husband was in jail that she had given up and gone back to her people in the East.

Richards also left the Harolsen place and showed up next at the home of Pete Anderson, a bachelor, who was homesteading a quarter section of land not far from the Harolsen place. The two men seemed to get along quite well for a while. Then they began to quarrel. Neighbors noticed it but decided it was none of their business.

Pete Anderson appeared at a neighbor's place one day feeling sick. The neighbors felt sure that he had been poisoned. They doctored him and suggested that he not go back

home till someone checked on Richards. But since he was feeling better, Anderson went back home.

The next day the neighbors thought they should check on him to see how he was recovering. They drove over to the Anderson place. Richards was in the yard with Anderson's team, a mule and a gray horse, hitched to the wagon. Anderson was nowhere in sight.

When asked where Anderson was, Richards told them that he had gone to a neighbor's place and would be back in a few minutes. Richards invited them to go inside and wait for him. They accepted the invitation.

They found the inside of the house a shambles. They rationalized that they couldn't expect two bachelors to have a spic-and-span house. Looking out the window, they saw that Richards had tied the mule to the wagon and was riding away on the gray horse.

With growing suspicion, they considered pursuing Richards but they couldn't think of any valid reason. Instead, they went to the nearest neighbors, looking for Anderson. They hadn't seen him.

By now their suspicions were soaring. Both groups of neighbors returned to Anderson's house and began a systematic search of the place. Some checked the barn and outbuildings, others the house. Two men went into the cellar where the winter's coal supply was kept. It was the ninth of December and the pile of coal was still big, ready for the winter ahead. Observing that it had obviously been pushed around, the men began shoving it aside. Under the coal, they found fresh dirt and in a shallow grave, the body of Pete Anderson. His crushed skull told them he had been beaten to death with something heavy.

Now they wished they had gone after Richards when he first left. But another thought hit them. What about Mrs. Harolsen and her four children? They went directly to the Harolsen place and began a search. It was not such a long search this time. They found the bodies buried in a strawstack. Mrs.

Harolsen and her two oldest daughters had been killed with a heavy object of some kind. The third girl, Mabel, appeared to have been choked to death and the baby Jessie's head was smashed.

Knowing now the kind of murderer they were after, they went into Kearney to the sheriff of Buffalo County, David Anderson (no relation to the murdered man, Pete Anderson). Although the murders had happened in Kearney County, Sheriff Anderson of Buffalo County took the job of finding Samuel Richards.

There was only one way that a man could get out of the country fast and that was the railroad. Anderson was sure that Richards had chosen that means of escape. He must have known that neighbors would eventually find Pete Anderson's body. Even if they didn't, they'd get suspicious of his disappearance along with the sudden vanishing of the entire Harolsen family.

At first, it seemed logical that Richards would go west but the few clues that turned up indicated he had gone east, probably thinking he could hide better among crowds than in the vast empty spaces of the West.

The Pinkerton Detective Agency sent a man to accompany the sheriff. They left Kearney on the Union Pacific Railroad. Occasionally they found clues of Richards' passing but quickly lost the trail each time. The only thing they knew for sure was that he had fled east. They kept searching. The brutal murdered of so many people could not go unpunished.

In Steubenville, Ohio, they picked up his trail again—this time it was hot. A man fitting Richards' description had been seen just recently in town. Sheriff Anderson had grown a full beard since leaving Kearney nearly three months before so he was confident Richards wouldn't recognize him. The sheriff had the advantage of knowing who he was looking for while Richards would hardly expect to see the sheriff of Buffalo County, Nebraska, in Ohio.

The sheriff spotted Richards in a city park,

strolling with a young woman. The Pinkerton agent circled around to get ahead of the couple while the sheriff move up behind them. The couple paid no attention to the bearded man until the sheriff yelled for Richards to put up his hands. Richards wheeled toward him but just then the Pinkerton agent called from the other side. Surrounded Richards put up no fight. He might even have thought it was all a mistake since he didn't recognize either man.

The Pinkerton agent slapped handcuffs on Richards. Then they took him and the woman to police headquarters for questioning. The woman was furious at the two strangers for arresting the man she considered her best friend.

At the police station, Richards was confronted with the accusations of Sheriff Anderson. He recognized the sheriff now and, surprisingly, readily admitted his crimes. To the utter astonishment of the young woman he'd been strolling with he openly admitted that he had planned to get her money, which apparently was considerable, and then kill her. The woman's indignation at the sheriff and Pinkerton agent collapsed like a punctured toad and she left the station on the wings of fear.

When asked for details, Richards almost bragged about the way he had killed the Harolsen family. He had used a flatiron to mash the heads of Mrs. Harolsen and the two oldest girls, Mary and Daisy. He had strangled Mabel and had grabbed the baby by her feet and dashed her head against the bedpost. He had used a hammer on Pete Anderson. He also admitted that he had shot another Kearney County resident, a man named Chatfield, on March 15, 1878, just before he had gone to jail for stealing the watch.

The Pinkerton agent had finished his job so Sheriff Anderson returned the prisoner to Nebraska by himself. In those days the passenger service on trains was often in the caboose on a freight train. This was the way

Sheriff Anderson brought Samuel Richards back to Nebraska.

Word had raced ahead by way of the telegraph that Richards had been caught and was being returned to Kearney. The anger in the two adjoining counties of Buffalo and Kearney was still at fever pitch—long before the train was due at Kearney, a lynch party had formed. They had a rope draped over the cross arm of a telegraph pole at the depot waiting just for Richards.

When Sheriff Anderson arrived in Grand Island, about forty miles from Kearney, the station operator informed him that he had a telegram. It was from his wife, Margaret, who told him about the mob waiting to lynch the prisoner. The sheriff wired back to his wife to get a fast team and buggy and meet him at Buda, about five miles east of Kearney.

News of the waiting mob at Kearney reached the ears of the train crew who had as little use for the murderer as the people of Kearney and Buffalo Counties. They taunted Richards about how it would feel to dance on air and get his neck stretched. Richards' bravado, which had been in full bloom even after he was caught back in Steubenville, wilted and he shrank back in abject fear.

Meanwhile, as the train moved along the Platte Valley toward Kearney, Margaret Anderson got a fast team and buggy from the livery barn and drove out of town, making

sure those waiting for the train at the depot did not see her. She arrived at Buda before the train pulled in.

As soon as the train stopped to unload some freight at the Buda station, Sheriff Anderson hustled Richards off. Pushing him over to the buggy, he shackled his feet to the iron step used by passengers getting into the rig on the side of the buggy. Then he unlocked one handcuff, passed the chain around the iron bar that rimmed the end of the buggy seat, and locked it back on the prisoner's wrist. Richards was twisted halfway around with both hands and feet fastened to the side of the buggy; he could not possibly interfere with Margaret Anderson as she drove the team.

The moment the train crew saw what the sheriff was doing, they yelled at the telegraph operator to wire Kearney and tell the people that the sheriff was sending the prisoner directly to the jail in a buggy. They would have to intercept the prisoner at the jail.

The jail was made of limestone hauled from Kansas. Wooden jails simply would not hold criminals desperate to escape. So in 1874, Kearney had built the stone jail. No one had broken out of it and it was used not only by Buffalo County but by many surrounding counties.

The sheriff heard them yelling at the telegraph operator and did some yelling of his own, promising to take the operator to the

Passenger Depot in Kearney, 1923

jail and throw him in a cell with Richards if he so much as touched a key to send that message. The young operator backed off.

The sheriff sent his wife off with the prisoner. "Run the horses every step of the way, Maggie," he shouted. "Use the whip."

The sheriff climbed back into the caboose. The trainmen yelled at the unloading crew to hurry. As soon as the freight was unloaded, the engineer opened the throttle and the train gained speed as it pulled out of the station. The fireman shoveled coal furiously and the train roared ahead. If they couldn't send a telegram, they'd alert the mob in person. The engineer blew the whistle repeatedly to warn the people at Kearney station that something was afoot.

Maggie Anderson had gotten a good start on the train. The road, such as it was, paralleled the railroad track for some distance. When the train began to whistle, the team became frightened, as the engineer evidently hoped it would, but the noise tended only to produce more speed from the horses.

There wasn't much ground broken for farming yet so it was mostly open prairie the buggy had to cover. The flat prairie was no problem but the buffalo wallows scattered so profusely along the bottomlands stretching back from the river were potential disasters. To tip one side of the buggy into a wallow would almost guarantee that the buggy would upset. To hit a wallow squarely could upset the buggy but it was more likely to pitch the buggy down and then catapult it up with a tremendous jolt as it came up the other side. Either alternative made for a frightful ride. At the rate the buggy was going, swerving to miss the wallows was too dangerous so Maggie hit them squarely. Richards, shackled hand and foot to the buggy, screamed at Maggie.

"Maggie, stop! I'd rather be hanged to a telegraph pole than be dragged to death by a runaway buggy!"

But Maggie didn't stop. She whipped the team on, using all her skill and strength to stay in the buggy when it catapulted into the air and came down with a bone-jarring jolt.

Maggie had turned away from the railroad track some time before and cut across the pitted prairie because her only chance to beat the mob to the jail was to take the shortest route. The jail was a quarter of a mile south of the depot.

It was an uneven race. The horses were tiring while the train was picking up tremendous speed. It reached the depot at Kearney while the buggy was still over a mile from the jail. However, the train crew had overdone it. They had attained such great speed that they couldn't stop the train. The only brakes were steam brakes on the engine and individual handbrakes on each car that required a brakeman to apply. The train swept past the station like a tumbleweed in the wind. Even the shouting crewmen couldn't make the mob at the station understand what was happening.

By the time the crew had stopped the train and backed it into the station, Maggie had pulled the exhausted team to a stop in front of the stone jail. Deputies hurried out and unshackled Richards from the buggy. Richards let them know how glad he was to see them.

"I'd rather take my chances with a mob than take another buggy ride with Maggie Anderson," he declared.

The sheriff got off the train as soon as possible and headed for the jail. He was there with his deputies, armed and ready, when the mob came roaring down from the depot, frustrated and boiling mad. They didn't get to hang Richards.

Since Richards' crimes had been committed across the river in Kearney County, his trial for the murders was held in the county seat of Kearney County, Minden. Richards wasn't transferred to Minden, however, until the time of the trial.

Samuel Richards was tried for the murders of Mrs. Harolsen and her four children.* It was a foregone conclusion that he would be

---

*This author suspects, but has no proof, that the charge of murdering Anderson was withheld in case Richards somehow escaped the death penalty on the first charge. If that were the case, he would be tried again on the Anderson charge.

convicted. The judge sentenced him to be hanged April 26, 1879. A scaffold was built at the southeast corner of the courtyard, surrounded by a high board fence to keep out the curious.

However, the townsfolk felt a hanging should be a public affair. They came from miles around—when the hanging hour arrived, they simply pushed against the board fence and flattened it. Then they witnessed the hanging of the man who had so viciously beaten to death or strangled six of their neighbors.

There is a postscript to this story. According to reports, Richards was buried in a draw on Section 16, Township 6, Range 14. For some reason the local doctors wanted to perform an autopsy on the murderer's body but the sheriff refused. He posted a guard at the grave the first night. When no attempt was made to exhume the body, the guard was withdrawn. The next night, the grave robbers did their work and the autopsy was supposedly performed. According to one report, Richards' bones were later scattered on the streets of Minden.

The *Kearney County Gazette*, some years later, November 1, 1882, reported that Richards' skull was on display in the window of the newspaper office.

There were many other crimes in Buffalo and Kearney counties to qualify both Kearney and Minden as wild towns. One occurred after the turn of the century when their wild days were supposedly far behind them. On 28 April 1908 two girls were attacked at their home in Minden. They were left for dead and the house set on fire to destroy evidence.

However, the younger of the two girls regained consciousness and managed to escape the burning house, dragging her still unconscious sister outside, too. The older sister never regained consciousness. It was from the younger girl that the authorities learned the murderer was Bert Taylor. The fact that

Courtesy Nebraska State Historical Society
Samuel D. Richards after his hanging

Taylor had fled the county seemed conclusive proof of his guilt.

Taylor headed south on foot. Someone reported the next morning that he had been seen in the southern part of the county. From there he made his way to Franklin, catching a ride when he could.

The authorities almost caught him in Franklin. There was a circus in town that day, however, and Taylor avoided capture by mingling with the circus crew. If the sheriff saw him, he overlooked him as one of the men helping with the circus.

They completely lost track of Taylor then but they circulated a description of him all over the country that apparently kept him on the run. Eventually, it must have worn him down because on January 11, 1909, he surrendered to the brakeman on a train near San Bernardino, California. There is no record of whether the brakeman recognized him and forced a surrender or whether Taylor had simply gotten tired of running.

Sheriff Asa Ransom of Kearney County went to California and returned Bert Taylor for trial. He was taken directly to Lincoln and lodged in the penitentiary until his trial on March 25.

Taylor's defense was that he had met his exact double some years before and this double showed up in Minden the day before the crime. That night when Taylor saw the fire and got to the scene, he discovered what his double had done and, according to his story, he had set out to find the man, not to escape.

His testimony carried little weight with the jury. Taylor was found guilty and sentenced on June 3, 1909, to be hanged on September 17. The sentence was appealed, but the state supreme court upheld the district court sentence and the date of execution was reset for October 28.

The sentence was carried out in Lincoln on that date.

Chapter 4

North Platte

Reporter H. Stanley noted in the *Missouri Democrat* in May, 1867:

North Platte is a gay frontier hamlet; its citizens a motley crowd of construction camp denizons, roughs, and gamblers, emigrants but a few months from the countries of the Old World. Women from the dance halls, bullwhackers and teamsters would line the tracks to see the train in. Timid passengers, fearing to face so desperate appearing a multitude, were glad to follow hotel runners to a hastily constructed hostelry that charged a lot but gave little in the way of comfort. A gambling establishment was conducted in a large tent where games of chance never seemed to stop.

Existing on the expanding frontier, North Platte residents were ever fearful of Indian attack. Their fears were augmented when the telegraph to the East went dead after dark on August 7, 1867. It was a long nervous wait until they heard what had happened. No trains arrived from the East and the first news came in over the telegraph after the wires had been spliced.

The actual trouble was a few miles west of Plum Creek, about fifty miles to the east of North Platte. Indians had laid a trap resulting in the death of several men. This struck a chill through the citizens of North Platte. They were deeper into Indian country than Plum Creek.

On the night of August 7, a band of Cheyenne Indians, apparently led by the war chief, Turkey Leg, arrived at a spot where a section crew had been working that day. They piled several ties across the track and tore down some of the telegraph wire to fasten them in place. Then they lay in wait for whoever came to repair the telegraph line.

Back at Plum Creek, when the telegraph went dead, a crew gathered to take a handcar out to find the break and repair it. The six men, Handerhand, Murphy, Wallace, Kearn, Thompson, and Griswold loaded what they thought they'd need and began pumping the handcar up the track to the west.

In the dark, they didn't see the ties across the track. They hit them with a force that threw the handcar off the track and scattered the men and tools. The Indians leaped to attack. The men, although armed, were no match for the swarm of Indians. Some had lost their guns in the wreck; others were too surprised to use the guns they had.

Within a minute five of the six men were dead. The Indians thought they had killed them all, but William Thompson had been thrown clear of the handcar when it hit the ties. The Indians spotted him and as he tried to get up, they clubbed him down. Then they scalped him. But he wasn't dead. He was totally aware of the searing pain around his head as they ripped off his scalp but he made no outcry and gritted his teeth against the pain. One Indian stuffed the scalp under his belt but it fell to the ground before he'd gone more than a few feet.

The Indians had other things to do then. They had wrecked the handcar but they had their eyes on bigger game. With the tools scattered around the handcar, they unbolted the rails and using all the manpower they had, bent them up in a curve with the ends pointing back to the east. After using more telegraph wire to tie them in position, they settled back to wait for a train.

Meanwhile, Thompson had seen his scalp drop from the Indian's belt and crawled to retrieve it. Moving quietly, fighting the pain in his head, he crawled along the track toward Plum Creek, driven by the hope that he could get his scalp sewed back on.

A freight train was roaring up from the east with about twenty-five cars and a caboose. Four or five of the cars were loaded with provisions for destinations to the west. The engineer had no inkling of trouble. The headlamp sent out a feeble glare but it didn't pick up the barricade in time even for the men to jump.

The engineer set the brakes on the locomotive but it slid into the barricade with enough force to impale him on the throttle. The fireman was thrown against the firebox—he didn't survive the blow and the heat from the open fire.

The Indians pounced on the train, hitting the cars just behind the coal car—the ones with the provisions. They boisterously began jerking them out, loading some to take with

them and destroying the rest. That allowed the train crew in the caboose at the rear of the train to leap out and start running back to the east, leaving the dead engineer and fireman behind.

The Indians stayed at the site of the wreck, plundering the train. The crew saw a second train coming up the track, heading for another disaster. They succeeded in flagging it down and explained what was ahead. The engineer backed the train into Plum Creek and from there on back to Elm Creek where word was flashed to the east.

In the meantime, William Thompson had managed to get to Plum Creek. From there they sent him by special train to Omaha to try to get his scalp replaced. Although Thompson kept his scalp in a bucket of water all the way to Omaha, the doctor could not sew it back in place.

The railroad crew returned to Plum Creek the next morning. From the station they could see the fire three and a half to four miles up the track where the Indians were burning the train they had wrecked. The crew set a flatcar in front of the engine and

Courtesy Union Pacific Railroad Museum Collection

Union Pacific depot at North Platte

with armed men loaded on the flatcar, they proceeded toward the wreck.

The Indians were still there but the train crew had a sharpshooter on the flatcar. His first shot knocked one of the Indian leaders off his horse; the rest withdrew across the river. They had managed to kill seven white men, wreck a twenty-five car train and handcar, and had made off with enough supplies to last them for some time. For them it was a victory. For the white men, it fueled a determination to get the Indians off the land where they ran their trains.

About fifteen miles downstream from North Platte, an army post had been established in 1863. Its importance to travelers ballooned during the Indian wars of 1864 when it wasn't safe for man or beast on the plains of Nebraska. The post changed names rapidly during that period. First it was Cantonment McKean, then Post Cottonwood Springs, then Fort Cottonwood, and finally, in 1866, Fort McPherson.

Indians were a problem in the early days of the community. Mrs. Charles McDonald was alone in her home in North Platte one evening when she noticed someone staring through the window at her. A second look verified that it was an Indian. She was sure there were more out there. Being alone, she imagined every kind of terrible fate awaiting her.

Then she remembered being told that Indians were afraid of drunken women. She went to the closet and brought out a bottle of dark looking liquid. Keeping in sight of the window, she took a long drink from the bottle. After a second drink, she got up and wobbled about the room, giving her rendition of a drunken woman. Cautiously watching the window, she saw the face disappear and soon she was convinced that the Indians had gone.

She sobered up quickly. After all, as she reported later, molasses and water was not a very intoxicating drink.

The railroad brought in many undesirables who lived off the work of other people, usually by means of holdups. When the holdups and assaults became so numerous that the streets of town were no longer safe even in daylight, a vigilante committee was organ-

Courtesy Nebraska State Historical Society
Cottonwood Springs, near Fort Cottonwood.

ized to rid the town of the riffraff. Letters with pictures of a skull and crossbones and a rope with a noose went through the mail to certain individuals. Usually those letters accomplished the desired effect and the recipients vanished like dew in a hot sun.

The town finally got a jail and appointed a judge. It was thought that these deterrents plus the work of the vigilantes had cleared the town of the toughs who had filtered in. But one evening in February, 1870, a railroad section foreman by the name of O'Keif was held up at the depot of the Union Pacific Railway. O'Keif lost ninety dollars in the holdup.

By morning, the town had additional reasons for demanding action by the vigilantes; sometime during the night, the McLucas Jewelry Store had been broken into and plundered.

A thorough search of the store convinced Sheriff Nathan Russell and his deputy, William Woodhurst, that this had been the work of careful professionals. They hadn't a single clue to follow. Citizens who had begun to relax, thinking the undesirables had been

eliminated from their town, now demanded action either by the law or the vigilantes.

Later in the day, a chance find pointed in the direction that the burglars had gone. A jewelry tray that McLucas identified as one on which he displayed his wares was discovered some distance east of the store. The sheriff immediately leaped to the conclusion that the men had dropped the tray after pocketing the jewelry on their way out of town.

The sheriff knew of an old sod shack down near the railroad bridge. He'd also heard that some unsavory characters had been staying there. Guessing that those men might be the burglars, he took his deputy down to the railroad bridge and accosted the little sod hut.

They confronted two men inside who identified themselves as James Bates and F. Ward. They reluctantly admitted to the robbery of O'Keif but denied the jewelry store robbery. The two said there was another man living with them who had gone hunting. Sheriff Russell arrested them and jailed them in town.

As soon as the sheriff had the prisoners in jail, he returned to the sod hut near the

Courtesy Nebraska State Historical Society

A Greek laborer's bake oven, Union Pacific yards, North Platte.

railroad bridge. He and his deputy searched thoroughly and finally, when they pulled up a loose floor board, they spotted the stolen jewelry buried in the sand underneath. The third man had not returned from his hunt so the two officers took the jewelry back to town. There they announced that the stolen goods had been retrieved.

The vigilante committee was meeting in the log schoolhouse at that time, trying to determine what the vigilantes could do to guarantee justice. When the men heard that the jewelry had been found, which convicted the three men who were living in the soddy so far as the vigilantes were concerned, they decided quickly on a course of action.

They went in a group to the soddy to catch the third man of the gang but he still wasn't home. It wasn't long, however, till the lookout spotted a man coming across the railroad bridge. The men waited until he was almost across before they rushed out and confronted him. He had no chance to escape. The vigilantes were in front of him—if he tried to run back across the bridge, the armed men facing him now could easily pick him off. All he could do was surrender.

The vigilantes' leader demanded to know whether he was one of the gang who had robbed the jewelry store the night before. Terror filled the man's face as he looked over the men, one of whom was idly swinging a rope. Too scared to think of an alibi, the man confessed that the three of them had robbed the jewelry store.

The vigilante leader was not satisfied. He wanted a complete confession. He mentioned a letter the sheriff had uncovered with the jewelry. That letter suggested that the three men were part of a gang of thieves. The man admitted it was true. He was evidently expecting to be released as soon as he confessed everything.

But the vigilantes were seeking justice, not mercy. They were frustrated because they'd been sure they had driven all criminals out of the area. In spite of his protests, the prisoner was dragged to a cottonwood tree, the rope thrown over a convenient limb, and he was hauled up. Soon there was one less outlaw in North Platte.

But there were two more of the gang back in jail in town. The vigilantes hurried back. The jail was guarded, however, and the vigilantes were thwarted in their attempt to complete their rendition of justice. Realizing they could not get the prisoners without a fight, they found the judge and convinced him to hold a trial immediately for the two prisoners, even though it was dark.

The court convened in a fairly large building close to the jail. When all the formalities of a legal court proceeding had been taken care of, the prisoners were brought in. The building was crammed with people and surrounded by those who couldn't get in.

The evidence was presented; there was no question about the guilt of Bates and Ward. The sheriff and his deputy kept order and guarded the prisoners. What the mob intended to do if given the chance was apparent.

Then, just before the trial officially ended, the lights were suddenly extinguished. Confusion erupted. When the lanterns were relighted, the prisoners were gone. They were being dragged away by the mob. The sheriff was helpless against so many determined men.

They were headed toward a telegraph pole east of the jail and the next event seemed as inevitable as the coming of morning. James Bates, however, broke away and dashed toward the river. A half dozen men ran after him, shooting as fast as they could. Perhaps it was the way Bates dodged or maybe it was the darkness, but he got away. Disgruntled, the men returned to the rest of the mob.

They were all the more determined to hang the one outlaw still remaining and they accomplished that in short order.

The vigilantes soon realized that they hadn't cleaned out all the riffraff before because two dozen men climbed on the trains and left town over the next couple of days. They had seen the penalty for crime in the town and wanted no part of it.

James Bates, who had escaped hanging, was considered gone forever. However, later in the spring, a cowboy rode into town and reported to Deputy Sheriff William Woodhurst that he had found a body near Fremont Slough, southeast of town. Woodhurst investigated and quickly identified the body as that of James Bates.

Dr. Dick was summoned to determine the cause of death. The man had a slight wound but not serious enough to be fatal. The doctor surmised that Bates had plunged into the river to escape the pursuit and had become so chilled by the February weather that he died of exposure. So all three perpetrators of crime paid the ultimate price for their folly.

The mood in North Platte turned to one of excitement in January of 1872. Alexander II, Czar of Russia, sent his son, the Grand Duke Alexis, to the United States on what was said to be a goodwill tour, although there were rumors of personal reasons for the trip. The Grand Duke loved to hunt and when the Czar contacted President Grant about the visit, the president turned the arrangements over to General Phil Sheridan. Sheridan enlisted the army's top scout, William F. "Buffalo Bill" Cody, to make preparations for a big hunt.

Cody found buffalo on Red Willow Creek and chose a site there for the camp. He rode over to Frenchman Creek where Spotted Tail and his band of Brule Sioux* were camping, at peace with the white man. He invited the chief over to the camp with some warriors to demonstrate a war dance for the Grand Duke.

Reports differ as to whether the Grand Duke's train pulled into North Platte on January 12 or 13, but the welcoming commit-

Courtesy The Kansas State Historical Society, Topeka
General Philip H. Sheridan

Courtesy The Kansas State Historical Society, Topeka
William F. "Buffalo Bill" Cody

General George A. Custer with his wife Elizabeth "Libby" Bacon Custer and servant, Eliza.

Spotted Tail promised to bring turned out to be nearly a thousand. None of the Indians wanted to miss such a powwow. The Grand Duke considered himself to be roughing it but the Indians had never seen such sumptuous living.

The Indians put on a war dance that was almost too real for some of the old Indian fighters among the soldiers. They found a herd the next day and the Indians demonstrated their riding skills and how they hunted buffalo. The Grand Duke, who considered himself an excellent rifleman, missed his first six shots but then downed a big buffalo bull. He kept the head to mount and the skin for a robe to take back to Russia.

After the hunt, the party returned to North Platte. The Grand Duke and his huge entourage boarded the train to see more of the great West he had read about. North Platte settled back to its way of life without Grand Dukes and Russian royalty.

tee was well documented. A bevy of brevet generals met the Russian visitors: Major General George A. Custer, Major General E. O. C. Ord, Major General Innis N. Palmer, and Brigadier General George A. Forsyth of Beecher Island fame.

The Grand Duke had wagonloads of servants and supplies to take along on his hunt. His own tent was a huge affair with a carpeted wood floor. He had a Sibley stove *and* box stoves to fend off the cold weather. He carried plenty of champagne and caviar and all the delicacies he was accustomed to back in Russia. It was an incongruous camp for isolated Red Willow Creek that January.

The party lost no time getting to the camp site. They arrived for the first day of hunting on the Grand Duke's 22nd birthday, January 14, 1872. The one hundred Indians that

General George A. Forsyth

On January 19, 1875, a shooting incident, more humorous than tragic, took place at Foley & Senter's store. J. S. "Jack" Bristol, who operated a saloon a short distance away, was engaged in a transaction in the store when he got into an argument with another man over some business dealing at his saloon. The argument quickly grew heated and the men swung fists. Foley and Senter separated them and sent them on their ways. That should have ended the incident but Bristol, a little the worse for having sampled too much of his own merchandise, returned to complain about the way he had been mistreated by being thrown out of the store. There were five men in the store at the time, Stone, Murray, Dillard, Mackle and Jenkins, pretending to be customers but really enjoying the company around the stove.

Bristol was in an ugly mood, his resentment flaring. He became abusive and the men gathered around the stove decided it was uncalled for. They asked Bristol to leave. He refused to go so Dillard grabbed him and escorted him to the street. According to Jenkins, who witnessed this and everything that followed, there was no undue force used in ejecting Jack Bristol.

Bristol, however, took a different view. Dillard had barely gotten back into the store when Bristol took a large caliber pistol from his pocket and fired it into the store after Dillard. The bullet missed Dillard but came dangerously close to Jenkins before slamming into a barrel of dried currants.

Two or three more shots came through the door, not hitting anybody but causing a great deal of alarm. Then Bristol went around the corner of the store and fired the remaining bullets in the gun through the side of the store. One of those bullets went through the space vacated only a half second before by Mackle and then lodged in the frame of the stove.

That bullet put wings on Mackle's feet. He and Stone made a desperate dash for the rear of the store. Jenkins reported that Stone leaped over Mackle, who was in his way, and

FIRST NATIONAL BANK BUILDING, NORTH PLATTE, NEB.

Courtesy Nebraska State Historical Society
First National Bank Building, in North Platte, Lincoln County

took the lead toward the back of the store. But in his haste, Stone didn't select his course carefully—he slammed into a huge box of crackers directly in his line of flight. He bent double over the box and Mackle, attempting to hurdle him, discovered he wasn't the athlete he thought. He crashed down on top of Stone. Since he was on top, he got to his feet first and continued his dash for the uttermost part of the store. Stone was a split second behind him.

In the meantime, Sheriff Struthers, who was about a block from the Foley & Senter store at the time, dashed up the street to learn the cause of the shooting. By the time he reached the store, Bristol had run out of ammunition. The sheriff arrested him and lodged him in jail to await the next court session.

The Fourth of July celebration of that same year was marred by a shooting early in the day. Since the Fourth fell on a Sunday in 1875, the celebration was scheduled for Monday. On Sunday afternoon, Thomas Grimes and Michael Fillion had a vicious verbal battle in their backyard and bad blood between the two was still running thick on Monday morning.

Grimes and Fillion had been partners in a restaurant on Front Street for some time. They rented the building from Otto Uhlig, who owned three buildings in a row along the street. The three buildings had a common backyard. During the previous winter, Grimes and Fillion had put up ice in the ice house in that backyard, intending to use it in their restaurant business.

But Grimes and Fillion had an argument and dissolved their partnership. Grimes rented another of Uhlig's buildings, leaving only one door between him and his former partner. They shared the common backyard in which the ice house stood. Both men had a key.

Grimes insisted he had paid for all the ice so it was his. But Fillion claimed he owned half of it and kept using it in his restaurant. This led to hot words but nothing more. Finally Thomas Grimes had his clerk, T. H. Harnan, put a new lock on the door. Then he took the old lock and key over to Fillion.

This led to hotter words, especially when Grimes accused Fillion of selling some ice Grimes claimed was his. When Fillion couldn't get into the ice house he nailed a board across the door so nobody could get in.

Thomas Grimes had three kegs of beer keeping cool in the ice house for the big Fourth of July celebration. When he found his way blocked, he went to an attorney and asked what legal course he could take. He was advised, since he owned the ice, to pry the board off and get his beer but to be prepared for trouble.

Grimes took his clerk to help him get the kegs of beer. He ripped off the board that Fillion had nailed up, unlocked the door, and went inside. In the restaurant, Fillion saw what was going on and got his rifle. From his back door, he was no more than fifty feet from the door of the ice house.

Grimes was in the doorway, ready to take his kegs to his house. Fillion gave no warning. He simply lifted his rifle, sighted and fired. Grimes was hit in the right chest. He ran wildly toward the back of his house but sprawled flat before he reached it. He died within minutes.

Fillion, seeing what he had done and hearing Grimes' screams, guessed that he had killed him. He put aside his rifle and went directly to the sheriff's office and turned himself in. Sheriff Struthers put him in jail and went to interview witnesses to the crime.

There were several witnesses, the chief one being Harnan, who had been handing Grimes a keg of beer at the moment of the shooting.

The coroner's jury gave its verdict that evening: "Thomas Grimes came to his death by a feloniously leaden bullet fired from a gun in the hands of Michael Fillion on the 5th day of July, 1875, in the town of North Platte, Nebraska."

The next day a preliminary hearing was held and Fillion was sent back to jail to await action by the grand jury. The verdict resulted in a long penitentiary term for Fillion.

One thief apparently escaped punishment for what the editor of the *Western Nebraskan* (North Platte) considered a heinous crime. In the December 4, 1875, issue, he wrote: "Some son of a sapling whose love of fresh meat was greater than his love of honesty got away with a ham of buffalo meat Wednesday night belonging to Miss Rallory, which was hanging in the rear of her restaurant. Stealing fresh meat from a lady is about the meanest thing the police records disclose."

It is interesting to note that the McLucas Jewelry Store was burglarized again in March, 1876. This time the thieves, Frank B. Mason and W. H. Singleton, were not hanged by a lynch mob like those who robbed the same store back in 1870. They were caught but escaped from the jail by throwing pepper into the eyes of their jailor, Joe DuBois. They were captured again, however, and the record shows they were indicted in June of that year and received jail sentences for their crimes.

"Shot through the head; no hope." That was Dr. Dick's conclusion on first examination of Joseph Riley after a shooting scrape in Dave Perry's saloon on Front Street, Monday, July 24, 1876.

Riley and a gambler friend were in Dave Perry's saloon enjoying themselves when Riley told a joke on the gambler, referring to some incident in Texas involving a woman. Apparently the humor of the situation eluded the gambler. As Riley turned to go into the back room of the saloon, the gambler jerked out a revolver and shot Riley in the back of the head. Riley wheeled around in time to hit the leveled revolver before it fired again. This time the bullet went into the ceiling.

Riley left the saloon then and someone took him to the jail to have his wound dressed. That was where Dr. Dick made his examination. Dr. Dick's conclusion was that the bullet had entered Riley's head behind and a little above the right ear and came out above the right eye. In his opinion, the bullet had gone through a corner of his brain. He didn't explain how it was that Riley had walked into the jail on his own power.

Dr. Cargen came a short time later to spend the night with the wounded man. Since Riley didn't seem near death, Dr. Cargen examined him again and concluded that the bullet had not penetrated the skull at all but had traveled around the skull, under the skin, and come out above the eye.

Morning found Riley alive and actually feeling chipper. Both doctors agreed that, at the least, he must have suffered a fractured skull but if so, he showed no ill effect. So far as anyone could fathom, the attack was unprovoked. The joke on the gambler had not been that bad; neither was it meant to be anything but a joke.

Both Sheriff Bradley and Marshal Walker were out of town the night of the incident but Marshal Walker returned the next morning. He viewed the attack as vicious and worthy of the arrest and prosecution of the gambler for attempted murder.

The marshal began looking for the Texas gambler but couldn't find him. Then someone reported seeing the man flag a train some distance west of town and board it. Marshal Walker sent a telegram to O'Fallons but there was no one there to help. The marshal then telegraphed the deputy sheriff at Ogallala. Somehow that officer failed to make the arrest and the gambler got out of Nebraska without being brought to account for the shooting.

There were several attempted train robberies along the Union Pacific line. None had quite the succession of errors, however, as that which occurred just east of North Platte on the night of August 21, 1895. It was midnight when the train got under way out of the North Platte station that night—a half hour later than scheduled. There was a signal out to stop at Brady Island to pick up passengers. The entire train crew was in a hurry to make up some of the lost time so the stop for passengers was short.

The engineer that night was George A. Austin. Before they had gone far after their stop at Brady Island, the engineer and fireman were suddenly ordered to keep their hands away from any weapons. Austin wheeled around to see two guns leveled at him and the fireman. The men wielding the guns were coming over the coal car.

Austin started to slow the train but one of the gunmen ordered him to keep it moving until they reached the second curve ahead. When they arrived at that curve, the orders were to proceed slowly. He'd be told when to stop.

The command to stop came when they were even with some horses tied to trees. As soon as the train halted, one of the bandits ordered Austin out of the cab and back to the rear of the baggage car. There he was told to uncouple the rest of the train. That would get rid of the remainder of the train crew and all the passengers. But Austin was unable to get the cars uncoupled.

Austin straightened up and faced the gunman. "You'll have to shoot because I can't uncouple the train."

The conductor, curious over the stop this far from any station, poked his head out a window to see what was going on. He found himself within a few feet of a gun. He was told he'd get his head blown off if he showed it again. He didn't.

The bandit went back to the cab and brought the fireman out to help Austin uncouple the train. Together they managed to get the coupling unhooked. Then they sent the fireman back to the cab and forced Austin to rap on the baggage car door. When it was opened, the bandits leaped inside and made the man open the safe holding the short-haul valuables. After going through these and finding only a few things worth taking, they ordered the man to open the long-haul safe.

Here the bandits hit another obstacle. The safe had a time lock and there was no way anyone could open it until the set time had expired. The bandits were prepared for such an emergency, though. They went to their horses and brought back dynamite. They set it to blow the safe open and then all retreated to a safe distance.

After a long wait, one of the bandits started toward the baggage car. "It ain't going to go off," he said. But he reconsidered and backed off again.

The explosion finally came, rocking the baggage car. Before the smoke had cleared, the bandits were in the car, rushing up to

the safe. But the explosion had torn off only the outer door, leaving the inner door intact, still securely locked.

While the frustrated bandits were deciding what to do, the fireman up in the engine climbed down and uncoupled the baggage car. Then he threw the lever and started the engine, pulling only the coal car, and made a dash down the track toward Gothenburg where he could get to the telegraph and spread the alarm.

The bandits knew they had a very short time to get away. So they dashed to their horses, swung into the saddles, and spurred off into the night. They had gotten practically nothing for their efforts.

Their troubles were not over, however. They disappeared up a canyon to the north, avoiding the danger of crossing the Platte River to the south. They hadn't counted on the fencing the farmers and ranchers had done—one of the horses got tangled in a barbed wire fence and cut himself severely. So the two had to abandon that horse and ride double on the other. They rode that horse hard until he finally played out and they were left afoot.

Hoping they were far enough away from the railroad that no word would get out about them, they walked into the nearest town, which was Mason City in eastern Custer County. There they got breakfast. The railroad agent at Mason City happened to see them and decided they fit the description he had gotten on the telegraph of the two men who held up the train down on the main line of the Union Pacific. The section hands were getting ready to go out to work and the agent asked them to keep an eye on the men while he got the town marshal, a man they called "Rattlesnake Pete." Before the marshal arrived, the men had left the restaurant and headed down the railroad tracks, still on foot.

The marshal rounded up a posse and followed them. Some distance out of town, the two men decided to take a dip in the stream and refresh themselves. The marshal and his posse caught up with them there and Rattlesnake Pete ordered them out of the water. When one of the bandits reached for his pants, the marshal told him he'd be a dead man if he touched his clothes. Not until he had examined the clothing carefully and removed anything that could be used as a weapon did the marshal allow the two men to dress.

The two hard luck bandits were taken to Grand Island on the train. From there, they were shipped back to North Platte to stand trial. It happened that court was in session when they arrived and the two were very quickly sentenced to ten years in the penitentiary for their foolhardy escapade.

Vernon Connett was twenty-one, too young to die. His wife was just nineteen, too young to be left a widow with a tiny baby. Yet that was the way it was decreed by a thief who killed in order to steal.

Connett grew up on a farm near Bird City, Kansas. His wife had grown up near Benkelman, Nebraska. When they were married, they lived on the family farm. Love was young and so were they.

When their baby was born, the mother failed to regain her health and the doctor advised taking her somewhere to be outdoors, so Vernon planned a trip to visit relatives in Logan County, Nebraska, just north of North Platte. He readied the wagon for the trip and set out with the fine team of horses his father had given him.

First to Benkelman, then Trenton, McCook, Wellfleet and finally North Platte. They had left home on July 25, 1914, and arrived in North Platte the morning of July 31. They had intended to reach the town the night before but a heavy rain storm had forced them to camp a few miles south of town.

It was in North Platte that Vernon met Roy Roberts, another twenty-one-year-old man. Roberts was very friendly and Vernon was in a strange town. He welcomed any help this new friend could give him.

Roy Roberts was a pleasant looking man and seemed sincere in his efforts to help the young couple. Neither of the Connetts suspected that he had an eye for their fine team of horses.

He suggested that the two go out to the Sund dairy ranch, a few miles west of town. Roberts' mother and stepfather worked there. Everything seemed to be going so well that Vernon Connett and his wife were willing to follow any suggestion Roberts made.

Robert's said there were jobs to be had in haying along the Platte River to the west, and since Vernon was very short of funds, he might work for a while before going on to his destination. This met with the approval of the Connetts. However, Mrs. Connett, being so weak, might find the situation bad for her health so Roberts suggested that she go back home.

Mrs. Connett had an aunt in Mason City and she chose to go there. It would be next to impossible to go back home. There were no railroads running in that direction. She could get to Mason City by train, making only one change.

Saturday morning, August 1, Vernon and Roberts took her to the depot in North Platte and bought the ticket to Mason City for her. Vernon promised that as soon as he made some money, he'd send for her and they'd go on to Logan County. A storm came up while they were waiting for the train in North Platte so Vernon and Roberts decided they'd better try to get back to the Sund ranch before the storm broke. They left Vernon's wife and baby at the depot. Mrs. Connett would never see her husband again.

On Sunday, Roberts and Vernon prepared to leave the Sund ranch and go west to Hershey and possibly Sutherland to find work on one of the ranches. Roberts' stepfather, Charles Clayton, had told them there was work to be had up there. The two didn't get started until nearly evening, taking Vernon's wagon and fine team.

Monday morning Roy Roberts appeared at Hershey, west of North Platte, and sold the team and wagon, pocketing the money.

Roberts had a colorful history for one so young. A couple of years before, he had gained the confidence of an old soldier in Grand Island. After the old fellow had reached the point where he would follow Roberts anywhere, Roberts coaxed him into a dark alley and hit him over the head with a short iron rod. After robbing him of what he had, he left him in the alley, thinking he was dead.

However, the old man wasn't dead and he reported what had happened. Roberts was found and sent to the penitentiary in Lincoln for attempted murder and robbery. He impressed the parole board there with his perfect behavior so they let him out on parole after twenty months of his three- to fifteen-year sentence.

He had been working for a man near Brule when he had taken the trip to North Platte to see his mother. While there, he met Vernon Connett. Connett's horses had taken his eye and he knew he could sell the team for a good price. All he had to do was get rid of Connett. He worked that easily enough. After that, the necessity of holding a job would be simply a case of fulfilling his parole conditions.

Mrs. Connett had received a card written from Hershey saying that Vernon was doing some hauling and that Roberts had gone on to South Dakota. But the handwriting didn't look like Vernon's. Still she didn't suspect then that it was Roberts' writing. After the card, she heard nothing. Suspicion of foul play gradually grew and she wrote the sheriff at North Platte. He began inquiring.

When Connett couldn't be found, the law began searching for his body. This task was to take a long time; everyone who took an interest in the case joined in the search.

Roberts was suspected and he was picked up and taken to Lincoln where prison officials questioned him. He told his story with complete candor, except it wasn't the truth. He was the kind who "could convince a cat that a bulldog was a mouse."

When the livery man at Hershey who had helped Roberts sell the horses identified Roberts as the man who said he owned the team and wagon, Roberts changed his story, saying that Vernon Connett and Roberts' stepfather, Charley Clayton, had gotten into a fight and Clayton had accidentally killed Vernon. It had fallen to Roberts to get rid of the body and sell the team. He said he had given most of the money to Clayton.

Further checking proved this story also false. Roberts was arraigned and brought into court. The hearing resulted in a trial date being set for January 25, 1915. Roberts changed his story a few more times until finally, on January 13, he told the officers where he had hidden the body, although he still insisted that Clayton had killed Connett. He drew a map showing how to find the body.

He was in the penitentiary then for safekeeping until the time of the trial. The next day the sheriff of Lincoln County, along with a couple of deputies, followed the map to the marked spot south of Sutherland. There they found the body of Vernon Connett frozen into the sand and water at the edge of the South Platte river.

On January 25 Roy Roberts' trial began. It lasted for some time. The jury deliberated through one night and then brought back a verdict of first-degree murder and fixed the penalty at death.

Roberts was sent to the penitentiary in Lincoln to await his execution date which was set for June 4, 1915. One newspaper actually reported that he was executed on that date. However, he managed to wangle a new trial, using the same skills that had convinced his victims to trust him.

The new trial was held on February 5, 1917. This trial was ordered on the grounds that the first trial had been held for the entertainment of the masses of people who flocked to witness it and not for justice. At the second trial, Roberts pleaded guilty and was sentenced to thirty years in prison. He was taken back to the penitentiary and re-leased again on parole on June 30, 1937. From there, he disappeared, apparently weary of working his confidence game on Nebraskans.

Chapter 5

Culbertson

Culbertson was the first town to rise out of the plains in the southern tier of counties in southwestern Nebraska. It was established in the summer of 1873. Its closest rival for the honor was Indianola, more than twenty miles to the east, also founded that year.

The county of Hitchcock came into existence too that summer and Culbertson, being the only place within the borders of the new county even resembling a town, became the county seat.

The county and the town were barely a month old when they were initiated into the reality of the wild area they had claimed. The battle of Massacre Canyon is well documented in history as the last big battle between *Indian tribes. There had long been bad blood between the Pawnee and Sioux.* The government recognized this and assigned specific areas as hunting grounds for each tribe but it could not conceive of people who were entirely nomadic and would not recognize any pencil-drawn boundaries.

The Pawnee hunted twice a year. In the summer they hunted for meat and hides that could be used for clothing. In winter they hunted for meat and robes. The buffalo's shaggy winter coat made the warmest of robes. It was the summer hunt that the Pawnee began in early July, 1873. There were 750 in the party. They hunted along the Nebraska-Kansas border, as far from the Sioux hunting grounds as possible.

By early August they had killed eight hundred buffalo, dried the meat and cured the hides. They were about ready to head back to their homes near Genoa in Nance County. On their last hunt along the Republican River, at the head of a canyon about three miles north of present-day Trenton, scouts told John Williamson, trail agent of the Pawnee who was traveling with them, that there were Sioux in the vicinity. Williamson is reported to have told Sky Chief, the Pawnee leader, but the chief shrugged it off. They were at least two hundred miles from the Sioux hunting grounds, too far for the Sioux to be a threat. The hunt continued.

Hardly had the hunt resumed when the Sioux appeared. They far outnumbered the Pawnee. Williamson was called on to parley with the Sioux and went forward under a white flag. The Sioux, however, realized their superiority and wanted no part of any peace talk. Before Williamson got all the way back to the Pawnee, the Sioux struck.

Sky Chief ordered the women and children into the canyon and they poured down it like water through a funnel. The men, vastly outnumbered, put up a stand that lasted only briefly. Realizing they were going to be annihilated, they turned and fled down the canyon after their women and children. Sky Chief was killed by a Sioux bullet in the first onslaught. Fighting Bear became the leader but there was no place to lead except in wild retreat.

If the Pawnees could have held a battle line, the retreat might have been orderly and the casualties fewer but the Sioux were too numerous and too well armed. Their shots at the fleeing Indians in the canyon were totally indiscriminate. Almost as many women and children were killed as warriors.

John Williamson had his horse shot out from under him. There was no way he could escape on foot, although the Sioux were virtually ignoring the white man. Williamson saw a riderless horse. Stripping the saddle off his fallen mount, he caught the other horse and threw on the saddle.

Mounting, he sent his horse after the fleeing Pawnees. Through the dust, he saw a small Indian girl who had apparently fallen from the back of her mother. She was sitting on the ground, screaming in terror, holding up her arms to Williamson as he approached. Leaning far from the saddle, Williamson reached for the little girl as his horse thundered by. His hand touched her fingers but he couldn't get a grip.

Starting to rein up to go back, he saw the wave of charging Sioux. If he went back to rescue the Pawnee child, both he and the girl would die. With pain like a knife in his heart, he turned back and urged his horse to its limit, leaving the little girl behind.

The Sioux divided their ranks. One wave followed the Pawnees down the canyon while the rest split into two sections, each following a rim of the canyon. When the Pawnees hit a narrow place in the canyon, they piled up like cattle shoving through a chute. The Sioux, on both canyon rims and crowding in from behind, slaughtered the Pawnees like trapped buffalo.

It was a miracle that the Pawnees escaped across the Republican River without losing more of their number than the sixty counted dead after the battle was over. Company B of the Third U.S. Cavalry was in the area and took a stand to protect the retreating Pawnees. The Sioux had their victory, however, and returned to the northwest from where they had come.

Although the Pawnees were urged to go back into the canyon and retrieve as much as possible of the goods they had abandoned

Courtesy Omaha World Herald
Otis Rogers Collection

Nebraska in the Making

in their flight, they were too frightened and grieved to go back to the scene of death. It was left to Williamson and as many settlers as he could muster, including John Kleven and W. Z. Taylor, to go into the canyon to bury the dead and recover some of the jerked buffalo, hides and saddle blankets left behind by the panic stricken Indians.

The hot August weather forced the men to bury the dead in mass graves, in some cases, simply piling the bodies like cordwood under the steep walls of the canyon and then caving off the walls over the bodies. Among the bodies was that of the little girl Williamson had tried and failed to rescue.

The local settlers availed themselves of the abandoned supplies of the Pawnees. Many families ate buffalo meat through the winter. W. Z. Taylor was building his store right at the time of the battle, the first building to be erected in Culbertson. According to John Williamson's recollection fifty years later, Taylor also made use of what the Pawnees had left. Williamson stopped at the one building that fall in what was called Culbertson. He described the structure:

"During my visit, I stopped at Culbertson and the building there, or shelter, as it might be called, had been made from buffalo hides taken from the battlefield and then stretched over some poles. It made a very warm place in which to live."

That summer John E. Kleven settled his family on a homestead close to where Culbertson stands today. Two men came to the Kleven home one afternoon. They had been camped on their ranch several miles up the Republican. The story they told the Kleven family was that the one man, whose last name was Bess, had suffered a sunstroke. His partner was trying to get him to Indianola, roughly twenty-five miles east of Culbertson, where there was supposed to be a doctor. Bess, however, was too sick to travel any farther so his partner asked if he could leave him with the Klevens while he brought the doctor from Indianola. Of course, the latch-

string was always out to strangers and travelers in his frontier country so Bess stayed while his partner rode on in a frantic effort to bring the doctor in time.

Bess couldn't talk but he was still able to get around. He would neither eat nor drink. Still the family was not alarmed until the next day just before noon when he suddenly became violent. He grabbed the pan of buffalo meat Mrs. Kleven had frying for dinner, threw it upside down on the floor, and turned to smash some of the furniture.

Mrs. Kleven rushed outside and called her children. They ran to the dugout barn and hid. When John Kleven and a man named Macklin who was working with him that day came home for dinner, Bess grabbed a gun from the rack over the door and ran into the yard to meet them. Mrs. Kleven ran toward their neighbor Gesselman's with her children to get help while the demented man chased the others around the buildings. Kleven and Macklin guessed that Bess had rabies. His partner hadn't suggested such a possibility. Even the open hospitality of the Klevens might not have welcomed him if they had known.

Someone finally found a rope and lassoed Bess much like a wild horse. Bess was tied to a post for want of a better place of security. He raved on until he died that evening about the time his friend and the doctor arrived from Indianola. It was learned then that he had been bitten on the nose by a skunk. The wound had healed but when Bess got sick, both men suspected that the skunk had transmitted rabies. The newspaper reporting the incident confessed that no one had explained what Bess was doing with his nose that close to a skunk. Bess was buried on a hill just to the west of Culbertson, the first burial of a white man in the area.

In 1874 Hitchcock County held its first election. Galen Baldwin, one of the earliest settlers, was running for sheriff. A man named Grimes was running against him. Baldwin called him and his cronies horse thieves.

Three other men named Jack, supporters of Grimes, were trying to intimidate the voters. There was Fat Jack, Long Jack, and Curly Jack. Baldwin had a man working for him called Eban. On the day of the election, Curly Jack caught Eban on the street and demanded "Who are you going to vote for?" He said, "Baldwin," of course. Curly Jack threw him down and threatened him with a gun until he said he'd vote for Grimes.

Jack's horse had gotten away from him while he was manhandling Eban and he went to catch it. Eban got up and ran to the store where Baldwin was waiting and told him what had happened. Baldwin expected Curly Jack to come after either Eban or him. Baldwin's wife had insisted that the best way to stay out of trouble was not to carry a gun— so today Baldwin had no gun.

Within a few minutes, Curly Jack did ride up to the front of the store, which was also the polling place, and yelled for Baldwin to come out. Baldwin shouted back for Jack to come in and get him. Anticipating this confrontation, Baldwin had found a three-foot two-by-four. He stood beside the door as Curly Jack burst in, a gun in each hand. Before Jack could locate his target, Baldwin brought the two-by-four down on Jack's head and dropped him like a clubbed rabbit. Dr. Vanderlace was called; he pronounced Jack dead. He was wrapped in a buffalo robe and laid outside because he was in the way of the election.

Later Grimes came by and asked to see Jack. When the body was unwrapped, they discovered that Jack was still alive. Baldwin wrapped him up in the robe again, put him in the back of his wagon, and took him home. He and his wife kept him for nearly two months until he recovered strength enough to ride out of the country. Two years later, Curly Jack (McCall) shot Wild Bill Hickock in Deadwood, South Dakota, and paid for that crime on the gallows.

On May 28, 1876, two men camped near the mouth of Bobtail Creek where it emp-

tied into Frenchman Creek, northwest of Culbertson. Henry Stewart, about twenty, was a big man while his partner, Hank Randall, only eighteen, was a small man. They had eight horses and three mules with them. They contacted William Doyle and Stephen Bolles who had a pony ranch nearby. They raced horses and talked horse trades. Doyle and Bolles, however, recognized the men as two horse thieves from a description a Kansas sheriff had spread around the country.

Doyle agreed to a trade with Randall, and took him off to one side while he got the money to complete the trade. The scheme was to separate the thieves and get the drop on them. But when Bolles tried to pull his gun on Stewart, the wily thief drew his own and began shooting. He disappeared into the darkness. Randall reacted to the shots faster than Doyle and he, too, escaped.

James B. "Wild Bill" Hickok

The two ranchers started out early next morning with reinforcements to find the horse thieves who had escaped the night before on foot. The thieves were aided by a morning fog which they used as a cover for recapturing a couple of horses. The chase led over the divide between the Frenchman and the Republican Rivers until the ranchers got close enough to force the thieves to abandon their horses and hole up in a side pocket of Massacre Canyon.

There were six ranchers in the posse now and they decided they'd charge the hiding place if necessary. Then Stewart was spotted and a volley of shots killed him instantly. They called for the boy to surrender but he fought on for a while before giving up.

Randall said that Steward had hired him to help drive some horses to Wyoming. He hadn't known they were stolen until that morning. He fought because Stewart told him they'd hang him if they ever caught him. One of the ranchers guarded him through the night but by morning Randall was dead. It isn't recorded how he died, only that he did.

It seems no one in Culbertson wanted to be buried with the horse thieves so they selected a site on some land owned by a settler named Crews. This hill was to the northwest of town, while the community cemetery was just to the northeast. Randall and Stewart were buried near Bess, the man who died of rabies. The graves were almost forgotten.

Culbertson was growing now. Horses and cattle were streaming north to stock the sandhill ranges in northern and western Nebraska.

Courtesy Mrs. Paul Crews

Charlie Crews' house, built in 1886 just a short distance from where the horse thieves were buried. The gravesites are on Crews' land.

The horse trail came right through Culbertson.

The cattle trail ran west, crossing the Republican about where Trenton is today. Herds stopped there to rest before the final push to Ogallala. The cook often made a trip to Culbertson to restock his supplies, and all the cowboys who could be spared from watching the herd went along. It made for excitement that the residents of the fledgling town could have done without.

An incident occurred in the late fall of 1881 that angered the community. Clinton Dill owned a drug store and bar in town. He was thirty-eight years old and one report said he had only one arm. His temper obviously was not handicapped in any way.

One evening that fall, several cowboys from up the river came in and spent some time at Dill's bar. Two of them were Texas Sam Esman and Long Tom Hill. The celebration got a little out of hand and the cowboys began firing their guns. Some of the shots pierced the ceiling. Dill's living quarters were upstairs and one of the bullets came uncomfortably close to his wife, Mary, and their little daughter, Nettie. Dill ejected the cowboys in no uncertain terms. Most reports said that Dill threatened to shoot any who ever came back into his store.

On Wednesday, December 7, 1881, Texas Sam Esman and a friend came back to Culbertson. Some reports say the cowboys were unarmed but it wasn't often that men went anywhere without their guns in those days. The report circulated immediately after the affair was that the cowboys went into Dill's place and apologized for the disturbance on their last visit. Dill seemed to accept the apology and even shook hands with them. Then, without warning, he grabbed his pistol and shot Esman, killing him instantly.

The ranching community was understandably enraged. Many of the townspeople took the same view. A mob gathered quickly and only rancher John DeLay talked the men out of lynching the druggist. The editor of the *Arapahoe Pioneer* reported the incident and expressed disgust that DeLay had stopped the lynching.

Dill was arrested and his trial set for March 6, 1882. His lawyer was Oliver P. Mason, former chief justice of Nebraska's supreme court. The trial was moved to Indianola to find a saner climate in which to hear the testimony. The change of scene didn't help Dill. He was convicted of murder and sent to the state penitentiary.

His wife, Mary, moved to Lincoln and got

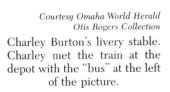

Courtesy Omaha World Herald
Otis Rogers Collection

Charley Burton's livery stable. Charley met the train at the depot with the "bus" at the left of the picture.

Judge Oliver Perry Mason, 1867

a job as a laundress to support their three children. She was close enough to visit Dill now and then. Dill's ability to adjust to confinement was inadequate. On August 24, 1884, a little more than two years after he entered the penitentiary, he found a knife and slashed his throat.

Less than a year after Dill killed Texas Sam Esman, Hitchcock County's elected sheriff resigned and Jack Wood, his deputy, was promoted to the job.

Early in October 1882 Wood and his wife went to Kearney to visit friends. While in Kearney, he got word that on October 13, Dick Belmont and Matt Simmerman had arrived in Minden, about fifteen miles southeast of Kearney. They were driving a herd of thirty or forty ponies which they corraled in a yard owned by Lewis A. Kent. They hired an eighteen-year-old boy, Charlie Collings, to herd the horses on the prairie around town during the days.

Knowing that Belmont and Simmerman were horse thieves and had stolen the horses they now held in Minden from J. T. Wray, of Hitchcock County, Wood rode south from Kearney to Minden and contacted Sheriff

Henry Lehmen delivering milk
in early Culbertson.

Charles E. Ericson, of Kearney County, asking for his help in capturing the thieves.

They learned that the two men usually got their meals at the Prairie Home Restaurant. That seemed like the logical place to try to take them. Wood warned Sheriff Ericson that they were dangerous.

The two thieves had discovered that Sheriff Wood of Hitchcock County was in town. One of them boasted that if Wood tried to arrest them, he'd die for his trouble. Rather reluctantly, Sheriff Ericson agreed to help Wood make the arrest. Neither sheriff expected the two to submit meekly.

The two sheriffs agreed that Wood would come in the front door while Ericson came in the back door. Both would throw down on the two outlaws the instant they were inside. It seemed unlikely that the two would dare put up a fight under those circumstances.

The plan might have worked but Ericson got cold feet and hid in a cave behind the restaurant instead of charging through the back door to support Sheriff Wood's play. Unaware of Ericson's desertion, Wood stepped through the front door of the restaurant after observing Simmerman enter by the front and Belmont by the rear door.

The two thieves were seated at a table facing each other. Wood faced Belmont; Simmerman had his back to him. Both men had their hands in their laps. Wood had his gun in his hand and he ordered the two to throw up their hands.

Both men obeyed but Simmerman had his .32 caliber Smith & Wesson revolver in his hand and fired it over his shoulder. The bullet struck Wood in the chest. He died almost instantly.

The outlaws leaped up and ran. A Minden man, R. B. Kelly, grabbed the first one to reach the door, clutching his gun wrist with one hand and his throat with the other and jammed him against the door post. The other outlaw promptly shot Kelly, killing him.

As the two men hit the street, they met Charlie Collings, the boy they had hired to herd their horses. One of the men shot Collings. The boy turned and fled down the alley and they shot him a second time. Collings managed to reach the rear of the Copeland Drug Store and stagger inside before he died. In less than a minute the two outlaws had killed three men.

They ran to their horses and mounted. Chris Larson, owner of the Prairie Home Restaurant, began shooting at the two men with his .22 caliber revolver. Belmont shot the gun from his grip, crippling his hand.

After riding through the streets, threatening anyone who showed himself, they left town, riding southwest. Belmont knew a rancher named Fouts near Oberlin, Kansas, who raised fine horses. By the time they reached his ranch, their horses were worn out so they stole fresh horses from Fouts's herd. Here they made a mistake. One of the horses they stole was the best horse Fouts owned.

The Fouts's oldest son, Charlie, about twenty, couldn't passively accept the loss of that horse. News of the shooting in Minden had spread through the country on the telegraph and Charlie suspected that it was Belmont and Simmerman who had stolen the prize horse. There was a reward out for the capture of the two murderers and Charlie had designs on that, too.

Charlie and a young friend, Frank Miller, went on the trail of the two outlaws. Knowing Belmont, Charlie figured they would make a beeline for a certain ranch in New Mexico so he and Miller headed southwest. The boys were daring but not foolish. In southwestern Kansas, a few miles from the Colorado border, they caught up with the two, locating an abandoned dugout where they had stopped for the night.

After dark Charlie slipped up to the dugout, untied the outlaws' horses, and led them away from the house. Then the boys put together a breastwork of stones and logs and got down behind it to wait for daylight.

At dawn, Belmont came out of the dugout. Seeing the horses were gone, he began searching for them. Charlie Fouts had a high powered rifle and he shouted for Belmont to throw up his hands. Belmont grabbed for his gun instead so Charlie shot him dead with the rifle. Simmerman came out of the dugout with his hands held high. The death of his partner had unnerved him.

Charlie Fouts took his prisoner and Belmont's body to Lincoln. There the two outlaws were identified and Charlie collected the rewards, both state and county.

Simmerman was arraigned in district court in Minden on December 14, 1882. At his trial he was found guilty and Judge Gaslin sentenced him to hang. Rich relatives came to his assistance and managed to get him a new trial. Again he was found guilty, but the case was carried to the state supreme court which upheld the lower court's verdict. Upon a writ of error it was appealed to the U. S. Supreme Court but was dismissed for lack of jurisdiction. Simmerman was taken back to Kearney to the jail there since Minden didn't have a good jail at that time. Simmerman's lawyer from Lincoln obtained a writ of habeas corpus served on the Buffalo County sheriff and got custody of the pris-

oner. Simmerman was never seen again. Some lawyers in those days, too, twisted the law to frustrate justice.

Charlie Fouts and Frank Miller were honored guests at a big reception in Culbertson and were given two hundred dollars for their work in capturing the horse thieves.

About a year later, in February 1884, another bizarre murder took place on Driftwood Creek, twelve miles south of Culbertson. It began as a simple fight between two brothers-in-law, Billy Owens and Elihu Currence.

Elihu was a heavy drinker. Even Eliza, Elihu's sister, didn't get along well with him. Neither was Elihu a popular man with his neighbors. They knew him as a lazy fellow who wouldn't work if there was any way to get out of it. He was always trying schemes to make money but wouldn't follow up on them if they required physical exertion. He was mean to his animals, even his favorite horse, a white mustang he rode everywhere.

Elihu planned to make a living without hard work. He had visions of a cattle ranch where the cattle would take care of them-

Courtesy Omaha World Herald
Otis Rogers Collection
Central Hotel, Culbertson.
(Note the rates.)

selves on the rich buffalo grass. He just didn't have any money to buy the cattle.

One day a young man from Pennsylvania, Billy Owens, wandered into the country. He had a little money and Elihu saw his escape from work. Somehow he wormed his way into Billy's confidence and they formed a partnership. Billy's money and Elihu's persuasion started a small cattle ranch.

Billy soon perceived his partner's nature. The money and the work were furnished by Billy; the profits would be taken mostly by Elihu. Billy might have dissolved the partnership if Elihu's sister hadn't come for a visit.

Eliza Currence caught Billy's eye the moment she appeared. One thing Billy needed was a wife and a home of his own. He didn't like living with Elihu and Jane.

It wasn't long before Billy and Eliza were married. Billy immediately set to work building a dugout down the creek. It was a short distance from the log house where Elihu lived with his wife, Jane.

At first Eliza liked it; it was her own home. But soon she tired of the hole in the ground where bull snakes could crawl in almost at will.

Elihu accepted the marriage of his sister to Billy Owens as a signal that now Billy was one of the family so anything Billy had also belonged to Elihu. That applied to the cattle but not to the work. Billy was a mild man and didn't like trouble but he couldn't take Elihu's bullying and the way he cut the bulk of the profits his way. He quarreled frequently with his partner.

Eliza resented Billy's growing hatred of her brother. And she hated the dugout. She began insisting that they leave the dugout and move back into the log house with Elihu and Jane. That Billy refused to do. He was as close to Elihu as he wanted to be.

One day the quarrel between Billy and Eliza became too hot to stand the strain. Eliza packed her clothes and moved up to her brother's house. Billy went after her and ran into Elihu. Eliza had told her brother that Billy had hit her but Billy swore he hadn't. The argument exploded into a fight. Elihu was big and fought mean and he whipped Billy. With a cut lip, a black eye and torn jacket, Billy got away from Elihu and sought refuge with his good friends and neighbors, the Charlie Knobbs family.

The Knobbs had a two-room dugout and six children but they made space for Billy. Billy was superstitious—he admitted he had visited a fortune teller in McCook. She had told him that he and Eliza would separate

Elihu Currence house, 1884

and that he would die with his boots on. She was right about the separation but Billy was reluctant to agree to the second part.

The morning after the fight, Elihu rode his little mustang up to Knobbs on his way to Culbertson. He was in an ugly mood and Charlie Knobbs couldn't get a decent word out of him. Elihu asked if Billy was there and then spurred out of the yard without waiting for an answer. Charlie realized that Elihu knew where Billy was.

A neighbor, Gus Anderson, told Charlie that morning that Elihu had said he was gunning for his brother-in-law. Elihu returned to Charlie's on his way home from town. Charlie heard him coming and went outside to meet him. Billy came out and stood beside him.

Elihu jerked his lathered pony to a stop in the yard. There were red streaks on the pony's flanks and sides where Elihu had raked her with his spurs. Foam and sweat trickled down her withers. He had a bottle sticking out of one pocket and it was obvious he was drunker than usual.

He swore at Billy. "If you ever set foot on my place again or try to see Eliza, I'll blow you to hell and back," he roared.

Billy was scared; his legs were shaking— but he wouldn't back off. "I'm coming up to get my trunk," he said.

Elihu whipped out his gun. "Where you're going, you won't need no trunk," he yelled.

Before Charlie could stop him, he fired and Billy staggered back with a bullet in his chest. Elihu jabbed spurs into the pony's flanks and the little mustang leaped into a gallop. Elihu stood straight up in the stirrups and threw the gun into a patch of sunflowers as he left the yard.

Charlie and Mary Knobbs lifted Billy and led him into the house where they laid him on the bed. With blood bubbling on his lips, Billy whispered, "I'm done for. Like the fortune teller said, I'll die with my boots on."

The nearest doctor was at Cornell, fifteen miles away on the Nebraska-Kansas line. By the time the Knobbs could summon him to their dugout, it was too late. Billy had lost too much blood and he died the next day, Valentine's Day, 1884.

After Billy died, Charlie Knobbs went to Culbertson and got the sheriff. The sheriff got as far as Charlie's place and took sick. Charlie was sure it was simply a case of nerves—he was afraid to arrest Elihu Currence. Another trip was made to Culbertson to get the deputy while Mary Knobbs put the sheriff to bed and nursed him through his sick spell.

By the time the deputy got to the Currence log house, he found only Jane Currence and Eliza Owens there. Someone had seen a man riding hard on a pinto pony but didn't suspect it was Elihu. It was then that a neighbor, Jim Frakes of Cornell, remembered stopping at the Currence place the evening before while looking for cattle. Frakes hadn't heard of the murder. He'd been puzzled to find Elihu painting black spots on his little white mustang. Now he understood.

A funeral service was held for Billy at Charlie Knobbs' place. Dan Matson, a homesteader preacher, read the third chapter of Genesis and said a few words. Then the wooden casket was loaded in a lumber wagon. It was hauled to Culbertson and then shipped back to Pennsylvania for burial.

About a year later, Charlie Knobbs read in a paper about a man in eastern Nebraska

Courtesy Mrs. Sarah Hook

Stone church south of Culbertson, 1879

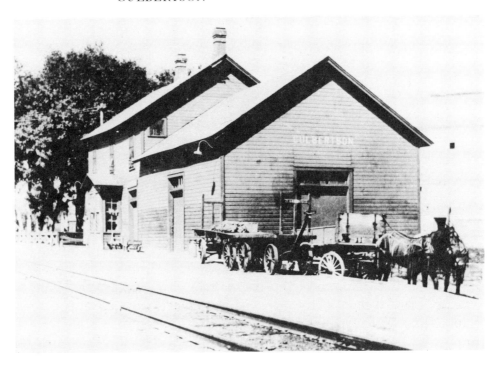

Courtesy Mrs. Sarah Hook
Culbertson depot torn down in 1973.

who had been executed for murder. Before he died, he confessed to a murder the year before in Hitchcock County. The name was not the same but Charlie knew from the description that it was Elihu Currence.

Many years later, William Stock, who farmed the land where Charlie Knobbs had lived, plowed up an old rusty gun that he believed was the one Elihu Currence had thrown away the afternoon he killed Billy Owens.

Chapter 6

Ogallala

As the railroad laid its glistening steel ribbons across Nebraska's prairie, it planted towns along the way. Some grew; some withered and blew away in the incessant winds. Sprouted in 1867, Ogallala gave every indication that it was one that would wither and blow away.

No one envisioned that a wild town would rise out of the grass along the north bank of the South Platte River—not even the Lonergan brothers, Thomas and Philip, who liked the area and became merchants and ranchers along the river. Neither did Louis Aufdengarten, who arrived in 1868 with the army as a sutler and returned the next year on his own and set up a store. His was the leading store in the little town for several years.

A few cattle appeared in the good grass along the river. Even some Texas cattle passed through on their way to somewhere else. But it wasn't until the railroad built some loading pens just west of town in 1874 that Ogallala really took root and began to thrive.

Settlers blocked the roads to eastern Nebraska markets so the trail had to move west. All the land west of the 100th meridian was considered unfit for the plow so the railroad people reasoned that a market established at Ogallala would thrive indefinitely. For about a decade they were right. The years, 1875 to 1885, were years that Ogallala would never forget. Andy Adams, arriving during that time, called Ogallala the "Gomorrah of the cattle trail."

By 1874 there were still only a half dozen buildings in town. Aufdengarten's store was doing most of the business. The Lonergans held such jobs as judge and postmaster. They were also running about three hundred head of cattle on the rich grass.

Men were beginning to realize the potential for making huge fortunes raising cattle on these vast prairies. The grass was going to waste and that was a sin no rancher could endure. But where would they get the cattle to stock this vast range? They knew the answer to that—Texas.

The call went south; the cattle came north. Overnight, Ogallala was bursting at the seams with a kind of man it had never seen before.

In 1876 the business district of Ogallala consisted of one street one block long and the businesses were all on one side of that street. A road called Railroad Street paralleled the rails. The businesses were on the south side of the tracks, facing north. On the corner of that one block was Aufdengarten's general store, second only to the saloons in the quantity of business done. Next to Aufdengarten's was the supply store started by the Lonergans, Thomas and Philip, but which they had sold before 1875.

At this time the entire Keith County had a permanent population of only 108. Ogallala, however, was being talked about all the way to Texas.

The two saloons, the Crystal Palace and the Cowboy's Rest, changed managers often but were always ready to wet the whistles of the men coming in off a dry trail. A little shoe store was next in line and then the courthouse which, reflecting the number of people it had to serve, wasn't large. On the end of the street was the hotel, Ogallala House, operated by S. S. Gast.

Across the tracks were the railroad station, section house and water tank. The few people who lived in Ogallala had their homes on the north side of the tracks. Phil Lonergan and M. F. Leech built homes there in 1876 and the pens west of town were expanded. The cowboys, expecting another Dodge City, were sorely disappointed but it was they who had made Dodge City wild. The cowboys were sure they could do the same for Ogallala and they succeeded.

As one cowboy described Ogallala when he returned to Texas in the late 1870s, "There's gold flowing across the tables, liquor across the bars, and blood across the floors."

One of the first murders in Ogallala happened in August 1875. There were herds from Texas grazing near town, awaiting ship-ment east. A young man named Webster who worked with one of the crews disdained the wild life that most cowboys followed. He neither smoked nor drank and his vocabulary was barely recognizable among the lurid words and phrases common among the drovers. 'Exemplary' was the word one editor used in describing him. That made his murder all the more shocking to the residents of the town.

It was concluded that it was Webster's refusal to join his crew in the boisterous fun and destruction that led to his death since no other motive could be found.

While the others were raising Old Ned in the saloons, Webster went down to the river to take a bath. One man named Woolsey left the others in the saloon and slipped quietly down to the river. When he reached the river bank just above Webster, he rose up and began firing his revolver, emptying it into the bather. All five shots hit Webster, one in the body, two in the lung, one

Courtesy Keith County Historical Society

Aufdengarten's Store

Courtesy Nebraska State Historical Society
Fire bell on Main Street, Ogallala

After the long trail north, tempers were often short and battles erupted sometimes without any great provocation. On July 7, 1876 such an argument exploded.

William Bland, trail boss of a herd owned by a man named Millet, was holding his herd outside Ogallala, pending their sale. Another herd, managed by Joseph Hayden, came in a day later. Bland decided to look over Hayden's herd to see whether he had picked up any Millet cattle. This was common practice—cattle lost off one herd were often picked up by a following herd.

Bland took his boss with him and rode over to Hayden's herd. Hayden met them and grudgingly agreed to let Bland look through the herd. Millet stayed back. Cutting out cattle was not his job.

Halfway through the herd, Bland spotted a cow with the Millet trail brand on it. He reined over to cut it out and Hayden objected. The two got into an argument, Bland declaring that it was his cow, Hayden insisting it wasn't. They agreed to talk to Millet about it.

Hayden was a little ahead of Bland and he surreptitiously eased his gun out of the holster. He wheeled on Bland but Bland saw the move and slid off his horse, grabbing his gun. Hayden leaned over the horse and shot Bland in the shoulder. Bland still had use of his gun hand. The two men emptied their

in the neck and one in the head. He was killed instantly.

Woolsey immediately got on his horse and rode away. Pursuit was quickly organized but Woolsey had a good start and no one was sure which direction he had taken. Webster was buried north of town at the foot of what would become known as Boot Hill.

Courtesy Nebraska State Historical Society
Cattle outfit, Ogallala. Frank Coker was wagon boss.

guns on each other. When it was over, Hayden was dead and Bland had a painful wound.

A coroner's inquest was held and the jury declared that Bland had killed Hayden in self-defense. Bland's injury was not serious and he recovered fully.

In 1877, Ogallala had more cattle and more cowboys and, consequently, more trouble. One friendly young man named Joel Collins brought a herd to town and sold it, receiving the money for his boss. Collins was a gambler and he thrived on games with big stakes. He promptly lost some of his boss's money.

Talk of gold in the Black Hills was rampant that summer and Collins and one of his men, a young fellow named Sam Bass, decided they could easily recoup their losses if they went to the Black Hills and tried their hand at the gaming tables there. It was a known fact, they had heard, that miners were easy pickings at a gaming table.

In the Black Hills, Collins played the games but he soon learned that easy picking did not apply to the professional gamblers who manned the gaming tables. Soon Collins and Bass had lost most of the money due their boss.

They returned to Ogallala, seeking some way to acquire, honestly or dishonestly, as much money as they had lost. They had tried robbing some stage coaches near the Black Hills but this money made only a dent in the debt they owed.

At Ogallala, Collins and his five men camped in tents west of town and roamed along the town's busy street, looking for an idea they could turn into money. In the Crystal Palace Saloon, Collins and his men planned a big robbery that would recoup their losses.

One of the men was dispatched to M. F. Leech's store to buy some cloth from which they could cut masks. Then they disappeared from Ogallala. There were six men in the crew besides Joel Collins: Sam Bass, Bill Heffridge and Jim Berry. There is some disagreement about the other two. Most reports name Jack Davis and John Underwood; this is generally believed to be correct. One source lists Sam Bass's partner as Tom Nixon but fails entirely to name the sixth man.

Early on the morning of September 19, about twenty miles west of Ogallala at a small station called Big Springs, the gang held up an eastbound Union Pacific train. This time, Collins and Bass hit the jackpot. The train was carrying sixty thousand dollars in twenty-dollar gold pieces. Even divided six ways, that made quite a haul.

It was the first robbery of a Union Pacific train and it caught the guards by surprise. The robbery went off as smooth as flowing honey. Nobody was hurt but the loss of six-

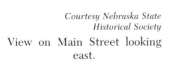

Courtesy Nebraska State Historical Society
View on Main Street looking east.

Courtesy Keith County News,
1976 Centennial Edition
Spruce Street, 1890

ty thousand dollars created an uproar all over the country.

The telegraph carried the news to Omaha where speculation attributed the holdup to Jesse James or the Younger gang. But one passenger on the train thought he had recognized Joel Collins. M. F. Leech was even surer of the robbers' identities. A brightly colored piece of cloth used as a mask had been found near the holdup scene; Leech recalled selling cloth like that to one of Collins' men.

The Union Pacific offered a reward of ten thousand dollars for the thieves' arrest and the return of the gold coins. Every would-be detective in the area charged into the hunt, but the bandits had disappeared.

Leech saw an opportunity to earn at least part of that reward—certainly faster money than he could make in his store. So he saddled his horse, took plenty of provisions, guns and ammunition, and set out. Logic told him the six men would head for Texas so Leech rode that way, too.

Up to a point, Leech was right. The six bandits camped on the Republican River south of Ogallala; there they split up their loot. They also split up the gang, going in different directions. Apparently Collins' original excuse for robbing the train to get the money he owed his boss in Texas was for-

gotten in the magnitude of the crime of holding up a train.

Luck was not with the bandits, however. Collins took Heffridge with him and headed southeast. Every telegraph station in the country had been notified of the robbery and a description of the bandits. When Collins and Heffridge attempted to cross the Kansas Pacific Railroad at Buffalo Station, (now Park, in Gove County, Kansas), they were recognized, trapped, and killed in a shoot-out.

Leech arrived too late to make an arrest—or collect any reward—so he turned to the trail of another of the bandits, Jim Berry. Berry had also gone southeast, apparently heading for his home in Missouri. In east central Missouri, at the town of Mexico, Barry was recognized. In the fight that followed, he was killed. Once again Leech arrived too late to collect any of the reward.

Leech returned to Ogallala discouraged. But people welcomed him, praising him for his ability to find and follow the trails of the bandits. At the next election, Leech was elected sheriff of Keith County.

Sam Bass and his partner made it back to Texas with their share of the loot. There Bass continued his life outside the law. He'd had a taste of easy money and he liked it. Less than a year later, on his 27th birthday, he was gunned down by the Texas Rangers during a robbery. Easy money for the bandits only led to early graves.

In the first five years of Keith County's existence, six sheriffs wore the star of authority. M. F. Leech didn't enjoy his position as sheriff. When he resigned, the perennial deputy, Joe Hughes, took over until a new sheriff could be appointed. Ogallala made a bad mistake when they chose Barney Gillan to wear the star.

Gillan was from Texas—he openly favored the cattleman over the farmer in any dispute. Nor did he restrict his jurisdiction to his own county.

When Print Olive, over in Custer County, offered a reward of seven hundred dollars for the capture and return to Custer County of the men who killed his brother, Gillan rose to the bait.

The two men were caught a fair distance east of Custer County. Nobody wanted the responsibility, though, of returning them to Custer County where Olive reigned supreme. Gillan accepted the job. He took them to Plum Creek where Olive was waiting with a wagon. Gillan made no effort to keep Olive from taking them. He even went along until they were in the county on Olive's ranch. There he took his share of the reward money and rode back to Ogallala.

However, when the hanging and burning of the two cattle thieves, Mitchell and Ketchum, was investigated, Barney Gillan's part in the incident became known. A warrant was issued for his arrest. Gillan heard of it and slipped out of Keith County to the home of a friend, rancher Russell Watts, near North Platte. He hid out there until he could flee the country. Nebraska saw him no more.

In late summer of 1878, Morris Wiehl came to Ogallala with a herd of Texas cattle owned by a wealthy lady, Mrs. Rabb. Acting as Mrs. Rabb's agent, Wiehl was assigned the task of selling the cattle. He quickly struck a bargain with N. P. Clark of St. Paul, Minnesota, a Missouri River beef contractor.

It seems strange that such a commonplace, peaceful beginning could end in tragedy 330 miles away on the Missouri River but it did. Wiehl and his cowboys, having sold the herd and painted the town of Ogallala a brighter shade of red, headed by train back to Texas. The train took them east to Omaha before they could catch a training running in their direction, south.

On September 7, while they waited for their train connection, Wiehl got into a game of pin pool at a billiard hall close by. His opponent was James Burke, a gambler and pool player. They played several games. No money changed hands; they simply kept a record of who owed the other money. At a dollar a game, Wiehl owed the gambler about three dollars.

Then they began to argue and things became heated. Burke demanded that Wiehl pay up and they'd stop the game. Wiehl was angry and refused to pay the three dollars. Tempers got hotter as both men strove to outdo each other in name calling. Finally Burke told Wiehl to wait right there and he'd be back. Wiehl said he wasn't going anywhere.

Burke left and Wiehl waited a short time. Then he went up the street to Collins's leather store. There he met N. P. Clark, who had bought his cattle back in Ogallala, and they stopped to visit.

In the meantime, Burke had returned to the billiard hall with his revolver but Wiehl was gone. One of the men there told him where the cowman had gone and he headed up Farnam Street to Collins's store.

Burke had a reputation of being a gentleman gambler. But there was little of the gentleman showing this day as he spotted Wiehl inside the store. Hiding one hand behind him, he entered the store and moved up close to Wiehl where he was talking to Clark.

Suddenly the peace in the store was shattered as Burke jerked his hand around and shoved the gun almost against Wiehl's side and pulled the trigger. The gun was so close

Courtesy Nebraska State Historical Society

"Mansion on the Hill." Built in 1887 for a bride who never came out west. Now a museum.

that there were powder burns on Wiehl's clothes.

Wiehl was hit in the left chest but he didn't collapse. Before Burke could fire again, Wiehl leaped forward and grabbed the gambler, one hand wrenching the gun from his hand. Burke was no match in strength for the cowman and Wiehl threw him back against a huge glass along one side of the room. The glass shattered, cutting Burke's head severely.

Burke broke away and dashed outside, angling across the street. Wiehl staggered outside, too, raising the gun to fire. But his strength gave out and he started to collapse. Men close by reached out and caught him and stretched him out on the sidewalk. He was dead within two minutes.

Some who saw the two dash into the street assumed that Wiehl was the murderer because Burke was covered with blood on his

Courtesy Omaha World Herald

William Paxton, an important rancher near Ogallala. The town of Paxton was named after him.

head and face after crashing into the glass. But witnesses inside the store told the real story. Among those witnesses was William Paxton, a rancher whose ranch headquarters was just across the North Platte River, northeast of Ogallala. The town of Paxton was named for him. He and others set the crowd straight and were witnesses at the official inquest held by Coroner Neville the next morning.

Burke had made a gallant effort to escape but he was caught on Thirteenth Street by a policeman named Byrne. He was taken to jail where a doctor attended to his cuts. Then he awaited trial in jail for first-degree murder. The results of that trial, if it was ever held, are missing.

For pure speculative excitement, September and October of 1878 topped anything that had struck Ogallala. At first, in mid-September when the news reached Ogallala that Dull Knife and his band of Cheyenne Indians had broken out of Fort Reno in Oklahoma Territory, the excitement barely touched the residents of town. Those few Indians would not get far with the army after them.

But each day the telegraph kept pace with the Indians and that was more than the army could do. Former Indian fighters claimed the only way to catch the Indians was to put soldiers ahead of them and cut them off.

This the army did, first at the railroad near Dodge City on the Arkansas River, then at the Kansas Pacific Railroad along the Smoky Hill River. The Indians broke through the lines at both places, fighting one battle near Dodge City and another south of the Kansas Pacific Railroad in a canyon called Famished Woman's Fork.

Neither battle stopped their flight to the north.

The Union Pacific Railroad along the Platte River offered the next good chance to stop the Indians. Major Thornburg was put in charge. He positioned scouts at various towns along the railroad to watch for them while he held troops and horses in readiness at Fort Sidney. They would take a train imme-

Courtesy Keith County Historical Society
Dick Bean, Paxton's ranch foreman.

diately to the spot where the Indians showed up.

Down on the Sappa in northern Kansas, the Indians raided farms and ranches and killed eighteen men. In Nebraska, south of the Platte, George Rowley was returning from Ogallala, trying to get back to the falls on Frenchman Creek where he lived. The Indians caught and killed him north of the Frenchman near Stinking Water Creek.

Nervous excitement was at its peak in Ogallala as speculation ran wild. People were guessing where the Indians would cross the railroad and asking fearfully if they might strike the town. Everyone made sure he was home in his own forted-up house when darkness fell.

But the Indians crossed the rails at high noon less than a mile east of Ogallala, as if showing their disdain for the pony soldiers who had failed to stop them. Word was wired to Sidney and Major Thornburg loaded his men and horses on the train and raced east to Ogallala.

The major unloaded his men and tore off in pursuit of Dull Knife's band. The people in Ogallala rested easier then. Now they speculated on where the major would catch up with the Indians. They were dismayed when Thornburg returned to report that the Indians had broken up into small parties of two to six men and were scattered over the hills. The white men at that time had a healthy fear of the sand hills between the Platte and the Niobrara. They'd been told that the blowing sand rose in high dunes. A man could get hopelessly lost within a mile of the edge of the hills and there was very little water anywhere.

So Thornburg turned back before he lost his entire command in those fearful hills. The Indians went on and it was the soldiers from Fort Robinson who finally caught them. Ten years later, those "fearful" sand hills were some of the best ranch country in Nebraska.

Boothill gained permanent residents in a rather offhand manner during the wildest years in Ogallala. One candidate applied for

a spot there when he went for dinner at the Ogallala House—sometimes called the Rooney Hotel because a man named Rooney managed it.

Two brothers named Moy were in the hotel ordering their dinner when Bill Campbell came in and sat down at a table near them. The Moys had come up the trail with a Texas herd; so had Bill Campbell. But there the similarity ended. The Moys had followed orders laid down by the town and checked their guns at Bill Tucker's Cowboy's Rest Saloon before going to the hotel to eat. Campbell had not checked his gun but he *had* consumed a large portion of the saloon's

National Archieves Photograph
Copied from "The Indians Last Fight," by Collins
Chief Dull Knife of the Cheyennes

merchandise and his reasoning was much the worse for it.

The waitress, Bertie Gast, came to take the orders of the Moy brothers and they quietly gave them, ending with an order of baked beans. This was too much for Campbell who was intoxicated enough to feel he had been insulted by the two who would stoop to ordering beans. He lurched to his feet, kicking his chair away.

"Just what I thought," he roared like a bellowing bull, "A couple of Yankee bean-eaters!"

Once on his feet, he continued to berate the two men, not bothering to find out that they were Texas trail drovers just like him. One of the brothers tried to hush him because his language was not meant for the ears of ladies such as the waitress.

Campbell, however, was not going to be denied the pleasure of thoroughly dressing down the supposed Yankee bean-eaters. The Moys decided to leave the hotel without dinner rather than be abused verbally by the big man. They had not missed the gun on Campbell's hip.

They left the table and went out into the street. But Campbell was not through with them. He followed them and continued to blast them for everything—from being overbearing Yankees who tramped on the Southerners, to being cowards afraid to face a real Texan. He bellowed at the top of his voice for everyone in Ogallala to hear that if they were too cheap to buy guns, he'd buy some for them.

The Moys still wanted to avoid trouble so they hurried down to the Cowboy's Rest to get their guns and leave town. Campbell saw where they went and followed them down the street. By now, he had worked himself into a frenzy, evidently convincing himself that those two men had insulted him beyond the boundaries of decency and he had to have satisfaction.

The Moys saw Campbell thumping toward the saloon, blood in his eye. As he neared the door, he drew his gun and charged inside, leaving no doubt that he was coming to kill.

The Moys had their guns now and when Campbell started shooting, they did too. They had the distinct advantage of being sober and they dropped the Texan like they

Fourth of July horse race (undated)

would a mad dog. Then they dodged out a side door, got their horses and dashed across the river to the bedding grounds of their herd. No one went after them. It had obviously been a case of self-defense. But the Moy brothers didn't show up in Ogallala again, not even to claim their orders of baked beans.

Others acquired spots on Boothill with no more reason than Campbell had. For instance, in July of 1879, Boothill claimed two cowboys, names unknown, the result of a totally foolhardy encounter. They had been arrested for a minor infraction of the town's laws and put into jail.

They couldn't wait until the next day when they would be released, but broke out of jail on Wednesday, July 9. The sheriff was using a crutch at this time and the boys apparently thought he was totally ineffective. Someone told the sheriff the boys said they could not be arrested again and the sheriff replied that there was no point in arresting them since their time in jail was so nearly up.

The cowboys, however, felt they had to show their defiance of the law. They got some guns, returned to the jail, and began firing into the building. The sheriff hobbled to the door, yelling for them to stop or he'd put them back into their cells. They retorted that there weren't enough law officers along the river to arrest them again.

The sheriff hobbled back and got his shotgun. Thus armed, he went outside and yelled again at the two to stop the shooting. They ignored the warning and the sheriff shot twice. One cowboy was killed outright; the other was carried into a nearby house to die. Although not named, the sheriff could very well have been Martin DePrieste who, through five terms as sheriff of Keith County, earned the reputation of being a level-headed, fair man but not one to back off from a challenge.

For several years, Joe Hughes was either deputy sheriff or acting sheriff of Ogallala, fill-ing in after the elected man gave up. Holding down the uproar during June through September was more than most men could handle, but Hughes wasn't like most men. In the summer of 1879, he faced a job that really required a small army. But the sheriff was either out of town or had "throwed up the job" as so many had and Hughes was filling the vacancy.

Word had come to town by way of the telegraph that some tough hands were on the train, coming to Ogallala to clean out the law. They evidently had run afoul of the law in Ogallala before and were looking for revenge. They were reported also to be horse thieves, and wanted in other areas.

Hughes, an old buffalo hunter and a good shot, made his way alone to the depot to await the train. When it rolled in, three men who answered the description of the ones who were coming to clean out Ogallala, stepped off.

Hughes lost no time on preliminaries. He simply shouted for the men to throw up their hands. Apparently they thought this was the place to start cleaning up the town. Instead of reaching for the sky, they reached for their guns. Bullets began flying toward Hughes.

This was nothing new to Joe Hughes and he calmly returned the fire. His first shot knocked one of the men down. A second bullet flattened another of the would-be town cleaners. The third man decided Ogallala didn't need cleaning up as much as he had thought. He dived between two cars of the waiting train and disappeared on the far side.

An examination of the two men on the platform showed that one had been shot in the head and the other in the heart. Ogallala was not cleaned up that night.

Martin DePrieste, after he became sheriff in 1879, did not take long to prove that he was going to be a good sheriff. DePrieste had come to Ogallala in 1877 from Texas. He was a small man, only a couple of inches over five feet tall, but wiry and tough. He was also a good shot—an essential talent for a

Courtesy Union Pacific Railroad Museum Collection

Old depot at Ogallala

sheriff of Keith County. He had not been in office long when word reached him that four horse thieves had raided a camp, stolen some horses, and were making their getaway south of town.

DePrieste went after them alone, knowing that horse thieves never give up easily. They knew that capture usually led to a short rope and a long drop.

DePrieste's horse had won many races against cowboys who thought their ponies were the fastest things on four legs. The little sheriff put his horse to his fastest pace and soon came up on the thieves. DePrieste seldom had to use his gun in town. Even the rowdies respected the sheriff's skill with his gun and avoided testing it.

DePrieste knew this would be different. Proof of that came with the bullets snapping back at him as soon as he came near the men. The range was long—the sheriff wait-

Courtesy Keith County Historical Society

Martin Deprieste

ed until he was much closer—risking being knocked out of the saddle.

His first shot dropped one of the thieves. A minute later, another bullet from his gun sent another thief sprawling. But then his luck ran out. A bullet from one of the two remaining thieves hit DePrieste in the arm and tore it up. He had no choice but to give up the chase. But two of the thieves had paid dearly for their defiance of the law.

Martin DePrieste would have a stiff arm the rest of his life but it wasn't his gun arm and didn't hamper his shooting. He remained one of the most feared sheriffs the Texas cowboys encountered.

Over the years that Ogallala was the end of the trail north from Texas, many of the gunmen and gamblers who plied their trade in those towns came to Ogallala, sometimes for only a brief visit. Ben Thompson was one of the best known and most feared of the gunmen who followed the gaming tables. He was in Ogallala for a short time. Although very little is known about his visit, the one thing that is well documented is the animosity he stirred up while in Ogallala. Ben was made to understand he would not be likely to leave Ogallala should he return. Several men were waiting to get a clean shot at him. This threat didn't bother Ben—he shrugged it off. He hadn't lost any love for Ogallala. Then the time came when he needed to go to the little cowtown on the South Platte and didn't dare risk it.

Ben was the dangerous one; his brother, Billy, was the one who was always stirring up trouble he couldn't handle. Ben had gotten him out of many scrapes in Dodge City, Ellsworth, and other Kansas towns. Wherever Billy Thompson went, he found some way to get into trouble.

He came to Ogallala in 1880 and, in short order, found himself in hot water. He made the mistake of locking horns with Bill Tucker, who ran the Cowboy's Rest on Railroad Street. Just what they argued about is lost to history but the rumor passed down through

the years claimed it was a disagreement over one of the ladies of the night who worked at one of the saloons.

Billy Thompson apparently came out second best in the argument and since he was a hothead, anyway, he resolved to right the wrong done to him. Walking into the Cowboy's Rest with gun drawn, he found Bill Tucker waiting on a customer. Thompson fired at him, clipping off part of his left thumb and the tips of some fingers. Tucker dropped to the floor behind the bar.

Courtesy The Kansas State Historical Society, Topeka
From W. B. Masterson's, "Famous Gun Fighters of the Western Frontier,"
in "Human Life," January 1907

Ben Thompson

Then Thompson made a grave error. Thinking he had ended the battle, with Tucker scheduled for a funeral, he holstered his gun and turned back up the street, taking his time since the fight was over.

Tucker had different ideas. He was wounded but not fatally. In fact, he wasn't even incapacitated. Grabbing the ten-gauge shotgun he kept under the bar to settle disagreements that threatened to get out of hand, he came out from behind the bar and ran to the door. Sighting Thompson walking down the street, he used his injured left arm as a brace to hold up the barrel of the shotgun and blasted Thompson, knocking dust from the back of his coat. Thompson dropped like a sack of beans.

Ben Thompson had friends in town though, and they tried to look out for his brother. They carried Billy into the Ogallala House and put him in his room.

Sheriff Martin DePrieste listened to the reports of what had happened and could come to only one conclusion. Billy Thompson had started the trouble by shooting Bill Tucker in the hand. It was attempted murder and DePrieste didn't allow that in his town. He placed Billy under arrest. Since Thompson was recovering from his wounds, the sheriff left him in the Ogallala House and placed a guard over him until he was well enough to be lodged in jail.

Angry talk buzzed around town. DePrieste's guard soon had a double duty to perform. He had to see that Billy Thompson didn't escape and he also had to ward off angry men who might try to take him out and hang him.

Some of Ben Thompson's friends got a wire off to him in Dodge City, telling him what had happened. Billy wasn't seriously wounded but there was a threat of lynching. Ben wished then that he wasn't blacklisted in Ogallala. He was one of the few people who thought a lot of Billy.

Ben went to his friend, Bat Masterson, who was also in Dodge City at that time. Masterson harbored no love for Billy Thompson but he was a close friend of Ben's and

for Ben, he agreed to go to Ogallala and try to get Billy out of there.

In Ogallala, he was recognized and DePrieste guessed that he might be there to try to sneak Thompson out of town. He warned his guard and told him to stay inside Thompson's room at all times.

Masterson felt that time was short. One circle of the saloons warned him that a lynch mob could be whipped up in a moment. He had felt that angry pulse throbbing through men before and knew what it meant. Bill Tucker was a popular man and he was one of Ogallala's own. No gunman from Kansas or Texas or anywhere else could come here and get away with trying to do what Billy Thompson had attempted. They'd lynch Billy as soon as he was able to walk to a telegraph pole.

Masterson had to get Thompson out of

Courtesy The Kansas State Historical Society, Topeka
William B. "Bat" Masterson

town quickly and without any of Tucker's friends seeing him. He had faced long odds before but this task bordered on the impossible.

Perhaps it is because Bat Masterson succeeded so well in carrying out his scheme that there are so many versions handed down as to exactly how he did manage to get Billy Thompson out of Ogallala without running into a lynch party.

Some reports say that DePrieste's guard in Thompson's room fell asleep and Masterson slipped the gunman away and to the train without being seen. Some say the guard was bribed and helped Masterson conceal his movements in getting Thompson to the train. Others say the guard was drugged. Only one report says that Thompson left Ogallala any way other than by train. He certainly didn't ride a horse. The shot from Tucker's gun had made horseriding impossible.

The most logical conclusion concerning Masterson's strategy is that Masterson shared a drink with the guard, only the guard's drink was drugged. That put him out like a candle in a high wind. It isn't logical that the guard would deliberately double-cross Martin DePrieste.

Getting the guard out of the way was only the first step. One report said that Masterson put Thompson in a dress as his lady friend and escorted him down Railroad Street and on to the train going east. Another said everyone was at a special dance so Masterson had only to throw Thompson over his shoulder and walk down the deserted street to the depot. Regardless of how it happened, the fact remains that Bat Masterson did get Billy Thompson out of Ogallala on the train to North Platte. There Thompson recuperated before Masterson took him to Kansas in a buggy. Most reports say that they borrowed the buggy from Buffalo Bill because Bill Cody was a friend of Bat Masterson and Ben Thompson.

Mansfield Sheffield worked at the Cowboy's Rest when he first came to Ogallala. In later years, he enjoyed showing off a big clock he had in his home in Ogallala. The clock had a bullet hole in it. Sheffield swore that this was the clock that stood behind the bar in the Cowboy's Rest when Billy Thompson and Bill Tucker had their differences of opinion. That hole, he said, was put there by Billy Thompson when he shot Tucker.

Martin DePrieste had earned quite a reputation for iron nerves. Perhaps it was part-

Courtesy Keith County
Historical Society
Manse Sheffield's Saloon

ly because he was so small—not the big burly type that most people expected a lawman to be. He was given credit for facing down a cowboy who had already wounded him and arresting him without a fight.

It started on the streets of Ogallala when a cowboy decided to shoot up the town. That brought DePrieste out quickly and he demanded the cowboy's gun. Instead of handing over the gun, the cowboy fired at the sheriff. DePrieste was hit in the leg.

The cowboy jumped on his horse and rode for his camp outside town. The little sheriff hobbled to his roan horse and mounted. He trailed the cowboy who reached his camp before he noticed he was being followed.

It was a big camp of cowboys who had driven a herd up from Texas. The cowboy called on his buddies to help but they wanted no part of his argument. Shooting a law officer was not their idea of a good time. Seeing he was getting no support, the cowboy leaped back on his horse and rode away.

DePrieste followed, gaining slowly on him. The cowboy fired at the sheriff but missed. DePrieste waited until he got close and then fired one shot, killing the cowboy's horse. The cowboy dropped down behind his dead horse with his rifle.

According to the story that got back to Ogallala, DePrieste dismounted and began walking toward the cowboy. The cowboy had his rifle aimed and ready but didn't seem able to pull the trigger. He finally threw down the gun and stood up. DePrieste brought him back to town.

There he found the citizens of Ogallala, who had seen the cowboy shoot their sheriff, waiting to string up the prisoner. They felt that anyone who would try to murder a sheriff deserved to be hanged. DePrieste stood his ground and warned the growing mob he would shoot to kill if they tried to take the prisoner from him. The mob backed off and the sheriff took his prisoner to Kearney to await trial there, a trial that netted the cowboy a term in the penitentiary in Lincoln.

The influx of cattle from Texas began to taper off in 1884 as homesteaders took land that included the trail to Ogallala. Kansas pushed its quarantine line to the edge of Colorado; Texas herds were forced to follow the state line on the Colorado side and then cut back to the northeast to get to Ogallala.

On August 6 of that summer, fire broke out on Railroad Street on the south side of the tracks and burned many of the business

*Courtesy Keith County
Historical Society*
Keith County Courthouse

Courtesy Emil Elmshaeuser

Early day Keith County home

buildings. Aufdengarten's store and a couple of the saloons were spared.

It was in one of these saloons, apparently the Crystal Palace, that Rattlesnake Ed Whorley got into a game with Lank Key. Key claimed he had won the nine-dollar pot and began to rake it in. Whorley said he'd been cheated and reached for his gun. Lank Key was fast with a gun—he beat Whorley to the draw and killed him.

Key left Ogallala in a hurry, some say just ahead of the sheriff's posse. Whorley was buried at the top of Boot Hill.

With the dwindling of the herds from Texas, it seemed logical that the violence would subside. But rowdy fun still popped up when inspired by false courage from a bottle. In February of 1886, four cowboys were in town—there was nothing to do on the ranch-

Courtesy Nebraska State
Historical Society
The little old sod shanty on the claim, Ogallala, Keith County.

Courtesy Elaine Nielsen

Stansberry hay crew

es at that time of year. Well after midnight, with "three sheets in the wind," they decided they wanted to get into another saloon but it was closed.

They slammed open the doors and began shooting every thing in sight. The proprietor of the saloon slept upstairs and the shots boosted him out of bed. Discovering what was going on, he left the building as if it were on fire.

The cowboys proceeded to demolish the interior of the saloon. But their noise had also roused the sheriff, who was still Martin DePrieste. The little sheriff showed up and the fun came to a screeching halt. The cowboys went quietly to jail where they had plenty of free time to contemplate how they were going to pay for the damage to the saloon.

With the end of the trail herds swarming in, Ogallala settled down to being a respectable ranch town. All memories of its wild past were buried with the men on Boot Hill.

But the town retained a touch for unusual behavior. When a fire swept through the town again, leaping from one frame structure to another, the old independent spirit came to the fore. There was no hope of stopping the fire till it burned itself out.

Gamblers in the saloons carried out the gaming tables and everything else they could. Seeing they couldn't stop the fire, they decided to carry on with the game they had started. So by the light of the fire, they dealt the cards.

Ogallala still had a touch of the wild town it once was.

Chapter 7

Sidney

Sidney came into existence in 1867 when the Union Pacific tracks followed Lodgepole Creek from Julesburg through the southern panhandle of Nebraska. Sidney Barracks, established in December of that year, was only a quarter of a mile from the Sidney railroad depot. When gold was discovered in the Black Hills, Sidney became the jumping-off place for prospectors, gamblers, and the usual camp followers who were attracted to the potential riches of a gold strike.

Sidney soon earned the reputation (which it shared with other wild towns) as the toughest town in the West. In 1882, one man who survived those years summed up what Sidney was like between 1875 and 1880.

For those years murders were so frequent in and about Sidney that the citizens became hardened and careless as to the taking of life, and but little attention was given to murders committed in drunken brawls. It was quite frequent in the dance houses here that someone would be killed during a quarrel, but no attention would be given to the matter further than to tumble the corpse into a corner out of the way until the dance and the amusements of the evening were over, and then take the corpse out for burial.

The *Omaha Bee* in 1899 had this to say about Sidney:

Eastern Space writers of two or three decades ago designated Cheyenne as the roughest town in the world, but it is evident that they never visited Sidney, else they would have located their blood curdling tales at the latter place, for there it was that crime ran rampant until the vigilantes took the law in their own hands and did some regulating.

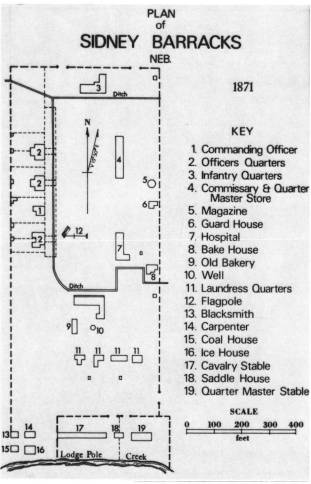

Courtesy Nebraska State Historical Society
Floor plans of Sidney barracks, 1871

The town did not get out of hand until the gold rush. For a while after the discovery of gold, the government made a good pretense of living up to its treaty with the Indians by making periodic raids into the Hills to throw out illegal prospectors. Sidney began to bubble that year of 1875. Most of the illegal prospectors headed for the Hills from either Sidney or Cheyenne.

It was in late October of 1875 that Charles Patterson and R. W. Parker got into an altercation not far from Sidney. Words became bitter; then bullets substituted for words. Parker was killed. Patterson was arrested and brought to the jail in Sidney. Parker was apparently well thought of or else people considered his death an outright murder. The crowd that gathered soon became a mob, bent on avenging Parker's death.

During the night, the mob broke into the jail, dragged Patterson out, and led him to a telegraph pole. Throwing a rope over the cross-arm, they hoisted him off the ground. The sheriff, coming up just in time to cut him down before he strangled, took him back to jail where he recovered from his choking.

The next morning, however, the mob was back. Overwhelming the guards, they took Patterson out of the jail and repeated the scene of the night before—except this time they stayed around to make sure their job was finished before abandoning the body on the pole.

In 1876, the government made another treaty with the Indians opening up the Black Hills to gold prospectors. Men who had foreseen the coming rush and had built and stocked stores in Sidney made fortunes as the trains disgorged thousands of prospectors. They outfitted in Sidney and headed north.

Not all who disembarked in Sidney were prospectors though. Many did their prospecting right in town. During the five years from 1876 through 1880, Sidney earned a reputation as the toughest town in the West; few dared dispute it.

At one time during that span of years, thieves became so bold that they met the trains. When the easterners stepped down, they were knocked over the head and robbed. After they came to, they had nothing with which to buy their outfits for going north. Many passengers who got off the train simply to stretch their legs during the stop

at Sidney were hit over the head, robbed, and thrown back on the train.

The law in Sidney tried to thwart these brazen robbers but there were so many and they used so many diversified tricks to rob their victims that the railroad finally ruled that the railroad cars would be locked when they went through Sidney. Sidney had been a meal stop but that was abandoned. Unless somebody insisted on getting off at Sidney, the train did not stop and the car doors remained locked.

The vigilante committee worked frequently during the years when Sidney was the jumping-off place for the Black Hills. Much of their activity consisted in giving warnings to those they felt the town could do without. More often than not, the warnings had the desired effect, but there were always those who thought they were not only above the law but tougher than the vigilantes. The last assumption was usually a mistake.

Gamblers who cheated and backed up their cheating with fast guns were particularly obnoxious to the vigilantes. They were sent packing and not many showed up in Sidney again. At least two, however, simply ignored the warnings and continued their trade.

The vigilantes took action. One of the gamblers was caught and used to decorate a

Courtesy Nebraska State Historical Society

Oberfelder's Outfitting Store, Sidney, 1876

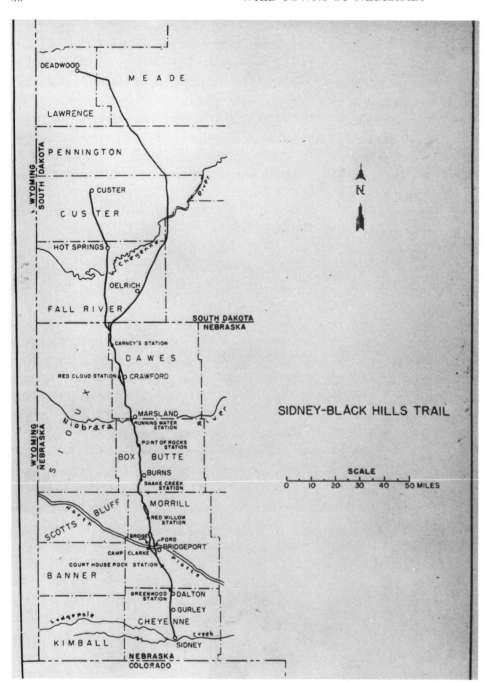

Courtesy Nebraska State
Historical Society
Sidney–Black Hills Trail map

telegraph pole. The other, a man called Cottontail, slipped away when he saw them coming and hid in a jewelry store. However, one of the vigilantes had spotted him sneaking into the store. They came in, politely invited him outside, made sure he didn't have a gun on him, and then stretched his neck from the cross-arm of a telegraph pole. Any other reluctant gambler who had been issued a warning suddenly remembered getting it.

The train that evening had more than its usual quota of gamblers on board as it left Sidney.

One gambler spent the winters at the tables in Sidney but was not under the threat of the vigilantes. His trouble came from another source. He was Efe Cole—he worked with roundup crews in the summer and spent his money at the gambling tables in the winter.

After spending his wages in Sidney one winter when the town was roaring, he took a roundup job with an Ogallala-based rancher. The roundup carried him down into the corner of Colorado. Efe was put in charge of a herd close to the South Platte River almost directly south of Sidney. His orders were to take the herd to a man called 'Pine Bluff' Tracy. Efe left with a chuckwagon and a cook plus three cowboys, one a black man.

About fifteen miles from the main cow camp they were surprised by a party of renegade Indians who had jumped their reservation. In the first assault, the cook was killed and also one of the cowboys. Efe yelled at his other two cowboys to make a run for it back to the main camp.

The Indians pursued but Efe held his horse to a gait that he could maintain for a long distance, warning the other two hands to do the same. Unfortunately, the white cowboy was shot out of the saddle first on one side of Efe. A little farther on, another shot killed the black cowboy on the other side. Efe kept going, holding his pace. The Indians' ponies began to play out and finally Efe got back to the camp where there were over fifty armed men, including some immigrants. The Indians took one look and retreated faster than they had advanced. Efe was given the name 'Lucky Efe' which he carried the rest of his life.

Shortly after the Joel Collins-Sam Bass train robbery near Big Springs, a stranger appeared at Walrath's ranch, east of Sidney. Charley Phillips was working on the ranch at the time. Mrs. Walrath was a pretty woman with a shady past. Her eyes were said to be steel gray and could bore a hole right through a man. Charley Phillips was attracted to her in spite of the fact that she was married to the ranch owner. The new man, Harry Dubois, was also attracted to her. Dubois had asked for work and Walrath had told him to stick around for a while and there would be work for him to do. So he stayed.

Friction soon built up between Dubois and Phillips. It culminated in a fist fight that Phillips apparently won. Dubois threatened dire things to Phillips but shortly recanted his threats and ostensibly made peace with him.

As if to prove his friendship, Dubois took Charley into his confidence and told him he was one of the Big Springs train robbers and had a cache of gold buried not far away. He even offered to take Charley there and give him some of the gold and they'd both be rich. Charley considered this a much easier way to make a fortune than grubbing away on a ranch for the next forty years, so he agreed.

Just before the two were set to sneak out and dig up the gold, Mrs. Walrath called Charley aside and told him not to go with Dubois. She said Dubois was going to kill him. Charley considered the warning while he twisted the blue kerchief Mrs. Walrath had made for him but the lure of riches was too great. He assured Mrs. Walrath he would take his rifle and keep Dubois ahead of him. But if anything happened to him, he made her promise she would send his body back to his mother in Illinois.

Charley left the house with Dubois leading the way toward the river where he claimed to have buried his share of the train robbery gold. It was the last anyone saw of Charley Phillips. People wondered about him but were told he had gone back to Illinois to see his mother. Then someone began to wonder why he would leave his horse and saddle with no provisions for their care. Questions were asked but it was always Dubois who answered. No one ever questioned Mrs. Walrath.

Then one day some hunters came by and stopped at the ranch. Mrs. Walrath was there alone—she told them a hysterical story that made them question her sanity. She said they could go out to the river and find Charley Phillips' body. He'd been shot once in the back of the head and once in the face.

He'd been buried by the river in the sand. She told the hunters she had seen all this in her dreams. Charley would point to the back of his head and then his face, reminding her of her promise to ship his body back to his mother if anything happened to him.

The hunters were more than a little skeptical but they organized a posse and went out to search the place Mrs. Walrath had pinpointed. They found nothing. Then one man saw a piece of blue cloth fluttering in the breeze above the sand. Investigation revealed that the cloth was clutched in a dead hand. Beneath it was the body of Charley Phillips. There was a bullet hole in the back of his skull and another in front.

No one in the posse believed in dreams and the sheriff arrested Mrs. Walrath for implication in the murder of Charley Phillips. Dubois was also arrested and charged with murder.

Investigations and questions finally brought out the story that Charley had followed Dubois about a mile from the ranch house, keeping Dubois ahead of him. Dubois suddenly wheeled and called a warning that someone or something was coming. Charley spun around to look and Dubois shot him in the back of the head. As Charley wheeled back toward Dubois, he was shot in the face. Dubois threw his body in the river where the water washed it up against the bank and eventually buried it.

The jury didn't believe that Mrs. Walrath had really had those visions telling her exactly where the body was and how the man had been shot. She was found guilty of manslaughter. Her sentence was ten years in the penitentiary. However, the supreme court reversed that decision and she was released. The court ruled there was no proof she had committed a murder or even abetted in its commission. The court did agree that she had harbored a known criminal but she had not been tried on that count so she was freed. She quickly disappeared from the region.

Harry Dubois was found to be a deserter from the army, identified by an army officer who said he had stabbed a fellow soldier. He was taken back to Montana and tried by court martial. He was sentenced to a long term in prison.

In 1877 and 1878 when Sidney was close to the peak of its boisterous existence, robberies were so prevalent that people were

Courtesy Nebraska State
Historical Society
Solomon D. Butcher Collection
Street scene in Sidney, 1877

not safe anywhere. It was during this time that the trains locked their doors and refused to stop in Sidney. Men from the East were enticed into saloons and robbed openly. The saloon operators were getting their cut so they kept the victims in the saloon on the pretense of protecting them. When they were sure the robbers had escaped, they let the penniless men go, warning them it would be best if they simply left town without saying anything about their losses.

It was during those days that Doc Middleton first got into trouble in Sidney. He had escaped from jail down in Texas where his legal name was James Riley. That had been in September of 1875. He appeared in Sidney sometime after that and landed a job as a teamster.

Things went well with him under his new name and he soon had many friends, including some who wore badges. Those good times ended on Sunday, January 14, 1877.

He was at Joe Lane's Dance Hall that evening, staying in one of the two bars on the ground floor. Sunday night was 'Soldier's Night' at Joe Lane's and only soldiers were allowed to go upstairs where the girls entertained.

Some troopers had just returned from a three-month patrol and they slipped out of their barracks at Fort Sidney, planning on a good time at the dance hall. The girls were on the ground floor being friendly to all, even though only soldiers were permitted to go upstairs.

Apparently Doc was a favorite among the girls. One of the troopers, James Keith, took exception to the attention Doc was getting. He made a hot remark to Doc and Middleton gave back as good as he had received. A fight seemed imminent. The soldiers backed up Keith while the bullwhackers supported Middleton.

Keith swung first and knocked Middleton down. A free-for-all broke out between soldiers and freighters and Middleton was not faring too well. Then the lights went out.

Middleton used the darkness to jerk his gun out and shoot at Keith who was all over him. The bullet caught the soldier in the chest and he died instantly.

At the sound of the shot, the soldiers broke off the fight and rushed back to the fort to get weapons since they had come unarmed to the dance hall. Meanwhile, the chief of police was helping Middleton escape, apparently unaware that anyone had been killed.

The soldiers returned with their big rifles and began bombarding the dance hall. Fort commander Captain Henry Wessles recognized the sound of army rifles and ordered Lieutenant Hammond to go with the sheriff and stop the battle.

After stopping the bombardment, Hammand discovered Private Keith where he had fallen after being shot. Even the soldiers hadn't realized Keith had been killed. They just knew someone was shooting at them while they were unarmed.

By the time they decided who had shot Keith, Middleton was gone. And so were his

Courtesy Nebraska State Historical Society
James Riley, or "Doc Middleton," at age 20

days of trying to be a law abiding citizen. He had no chance of returning to his job as a teamster freighting to the Black Hills. So he turned to an easier way of making money, stealing horses. In the process, he collected some of the roughest outlaws in the state, including one with an especially bad reputation, Jack Nolan.

Nolan didn't ride with Middleton all the time but he was usually close by when Middleton needed a good hand. Nolan frequented Sidney during its wildest days.

He got into trouble one night when he'd been out with one of the shady ladies of a certain brothel. When they returned to the brothel, she learned that one of her friends, an Anglo girl, was in a room with a Mexican cowboy, Jose Valdez. For some reason,

Courtesy Nebraska State Historical Society
Doc Middleton during horse thief days

this infuriated her and she begged Nolan to kill the Mexican. Finally she dared him to do something about it. Nolan was not one to be buffaloed by a dare from a woman so he went to the room and knocked, demanding to be admitted. Valdez blocked the door and refused to open it. Nolan shot through the door and hit Valdez in the abdomen. A short time later Jose Valdez died from the wound.

Nolan was arrested and taken to the Plum Creek jail to await trial, away from the highly emotional surroundings in Sidney. He escaped from jail, though, and returned to horse stealing, at times working with Doc Middleton. He headed a wild bunch called the Black Jack Gang.

Nolan had two cronies, Little Joe Johnson and Curly Grimes, with him when Deputy Sheriff Valentine of Dawson County came north looking for Nolan to take him back to Plum Creek (soon to be called Lexington) for his murder trial. The three saw Valentine coming and waited for him not far from some settlers who were laying up the walls of a sod house. The three surprised the deputy and took his guns and his money. Then they made him unsaddle his horse and took it, too, leaving the deputy to walk back carrying his saddle.

A young man, John Wright, who some described as little more than a boy, got into an argument with Ed McGrand on the trail just north of Sidney. Wright seemed to have forgotten the argument but McGrand, a Texan who doted on being tough, did not. Just before Wright reached the bridge across the North Platte River north of Sidney, McGrand overtook him on horseback. Wright was on foot.

Without any warning, McGrand drew his revolver and shot Wright, hitting him in the chest and angling down, coming out above the opposite hip. McGrand then kicked his horse into a gallop and disappeared.

Dr. Munn was called from Sidney to tend the wounded man but there wasn't much he

Pratt and Ferris freighting train on its way to Black Hills from Sidney.

could do. John Wright died. The search began for McGrand and he was finally captured. He was put on trial in December of 1878 for Wright's murder. The jury found him guilty and the judge sentenced him to the penitentiary for life.

Doc Middleton was now wanted over much of Nebraska, mostly for stealing horses. Various men rode with Middleton at different times so it was difficult to say who really belonged to his horse stealing gang.

In April 1879, Middleton and some men, including Joe Smith, left Print Olive's ranch in Custer County and made their way west

through Keith County to Sidney. They apparently were not recognized in Sidney until Keith County Sheriff Joe Hughes rode in with three deputies looking for Middleton. Some snooping on the part of the law located Middleton and his men at a place a little over a mile west of town.

Nobody had any enthusiasm for facing the horse thieves over guns so they set about laying a trap for them. The problem was getting the victims to walk into the trap. Charley Reed was in town and he was enlisted to help spring the trap. He had known Joe Smith back in Texas. Just what they offered Reed to play the Judas goat is not known

Camp Clark Bridge

Courtesy Nebraska State Historical Society
Some say this building was used for the Pony Express on the Greenwood ranch, where it is now located. Others say is was a blacksmith shop near Sidney.

but he rode out to the place west of town and renewed acquaintances with Joe Smith. He said he wanted to take the boys in and show them around town. Doc Middleton was suspicious of Reed but Joe Smith had known him back in school days so he trusted him.

Somehow Reed convinced Smith to leave his horse at the ranch and ride double with him. At town, Reed rode his horse down an alley where he said he'd leave him while they toured the town on foot. The trap was sprung in the alley. At the first sign of the ambush, Smith slid off the horse and made a run for the nearest building. He never made it.

With Smith dead, the posse decided now was the time to get Doc Middleton himself. They leaped on their horses and thundered out of town toward the place where Doc was holed up.

That, of course, was their big mistake. Even a man half deaf could have heard those horses pounding the hard road out of town. Doc was far from deaf and when the men arrived at the house, Middleton was gone. They pursued for some time but they had no chance of catching the horse thief. One thing Doc Middleton knew was horses and he always had one of the best for himself. His horse this night could outrun anything

the posse had. So although Sidney got rid of one horse thief, the kingpin got away.

Shortly after this, Charley Reed figured in another incident in Sidney—his last. It involved a well-respected citizen of Sidney, Henry Loomis. Loomis was just a few days shy of his wedding day.

According to later testimony, Henry Loomis and some friends were walking along the street when they passed the house where Charley Reed's mistress, Mollie Wardner, lived. She invited the men to come in since Reed wasn't with her right then. Loomis informed her that they didn't associate with other men's women. She took offense at the remark and sent a black man who was close by to look for Charley Reed. The black man found Reed quickly.

Mollie told Reed a man had insulted her and pointed him out. Reed ran after Loomis and hit him over the head. As Loomis turned, Reed shot him in the thigh, breaking the bone.

When Reed saw who Loomis was, he panicked. Evidently he had expected the man

Courtesy Nebraska State Historical Society
Mary Richardson, daughter of Henry Richardson, married Doc Middleton in 1879.

to be some newcomer in town who needed a lesson in Sidney's ethics. Reed turned and ran but Loomis's companions had recognized him.

Loomis was taken inside and Dr. Munn was called. He and three other doctors agreed that the only chance Loomis had was for the leg to be amputated. The doctors proceeded with the grisly job.

Meanwhile, Sheriff Sweifel, with Hugh Behan and several other men, started after Reed. They were told he had gone in a northwesterly direction on foot. When they came to a rocky area, they dismounted and proceeded cautiously. They soon spotted him hiding in the rocks and the sheriff got the drop on him. They disarmed him and took him back to town, locking him in jail.

An angry crowd gathered around the jail. Henry Loomis was a popular young man in town. Many people in the crowd had invitations to his upcoming wedding.

Through the night the sheriff and his deputies kept a sharp vigil but the crowd only stayed there. Everyone knew that the crowd would become a mob if Loomis should die.

The next morning, Saturday, the sheriff offered to try to get Reed to the train where he could be taken to another jail but Reed refused the offer. He was sure the crowd would never let him get to the train.

Then the blow fell. Henry Loomis died from loss of blood. The crowd grew and excitement rose as darkness fell. Sheriff Sweifel knew a mob of that size could easily overwhelm all the deputies he could gather.

About midnight, without the usual roar of excitement, the mob moved quietly toward the jail. Thirty or forty men surrounded and disarmed each guard. One man got the key and unlocked the cell where Reed was held. As Reed was dragged out of the jail, he made one plea.

"Don't hang me! Shoot me!"

The mob leaders quietly led him to a telegraph pole on Front Street, which was the main street of town. The leader asked for a vote of the crowd. Should Reed be hanged?

One man (later) reported five hundred affirmative responses and total silence when the leader asked for nay votes.

When asked if he had anything to say, Reed recovered himself to say that he hadn't known who Loomis was when he shot him. "I also killed five men in Texas," he admitted, "so maybe it is my turn to quit the game."

The rope was thrown over the cross-arm of the telegraph pole and somebody brought a ladder. Reed was given a choice of jumping off the ladder or having it jerked out from under him. By now, the inevitability of the situation had destroyed any hope Reed had and he climbed the ladder unassisted.

"I'll jump off and show you how a brave man dies," he said. "Goodbye, gentlemen." Then he stepped off into eternity.

Mollie Wardner was given some money and told to get out of town. She did. Henry Loomis's funeral was Sunday afternoon and it was the largest ever held in Sidney up to that time. Even the town band led the march to the cemetery.

In the spring of 1879, Smith and Ferguson, two horse thieves, were caught in Cheyenne County and jailed in Sidney, the county seat. They managed to break out of jail and escape, heading southeast. They were also wanted in Lincoln County so they veered away from North Platte.

The two might have escaped the law successfully had their true natures not overcome their common sense. In Furnas County in southern Nebraska, they caught a ride to Arapahoe with a farmer in his wagon. The two had no money and eating without money was not easy.

Seeing an opportunity to get some hard cash, the two men knocked out the farmer and robbed him. They left him and hurried toward town, determined to buy food.

Neighbors, however, found the farmer and revived him. He told them what had happened. In high indignation, they rode after the two thieves. Catching up, they quickly dispatched them, saving the law the work and expense of doing the same job legally.

Paradoxically, the escape of the two thieves from the Sidney jail speeded up the building of a new jail there.

After Doc Middleton was arrested in the fall in 1879, tried in Cheyenne, and sentenced to the penitentiary in Lincoln, he was brought from Cheyenne to Lincoln by Warden Nobes. It would have been an uneventful trip if the train had not gone through Sidney. At Sidney, when the train stopped, four men with hats drawn far down over their faces, boarded the train and began scanning the faces of the passengers.

They recognized Nobes but Middleton was not with him. They confronted the warden, inquiring where Middleton was. Nobes stood up with his hands on his guns and told the men to leave. They said they wanted no trouble, only Doc Middleton.

Nobes recognized the leader of the men as one of the biggest ranchers in the area. Knowing he had likely suffered a great deal at the hands of Middleton, Nobes knew what he wanted with the prisoner. Reluctantly the men left but they threatened to get Middleton, one way or another.

Nobes knew Sidney's reputation for taking the law into its own hands. He ordered the conductor to find a safe place for him and his prisoner. The conductor suggested the last car on the train. Nobes got Middleton out of the bunk where he had been lying, listening to all that had gone on. Taking his prisoner to the last car, Nobes closed and locked the doors, darkened the windows and put out all the lights.

At the next station beyond Sidney, the train was boarded by over a dozen men, evidently alerted by telegraph from Sidney. They walked slowly through the train, scrutinizing every face. When they failed to find either Doc Middleton or the warden, Nobes, they turned to one of the train crew, demanding to know whether Middleton was on the train. They were told that Nobes and Middleton had gotten off at Sidney.

Convinced Middleton had slipped through their fingers, they left the train in disgust. The train pulled out and rumbled on to Lincoln, carrying Doc Middleton safely to prison. Sidney had failed in its mission to rid the state of a bad tormentor of the ranchers.

Sidney's wildest days were from 1876 to 1878. In 1876 and 1877, the sheriff of Chey-

*Courtesy Nebraska State
Historical Society*
Gold storage vault, Black Hills
Stage Lines, Sidney.

enne County was Cornelius McCarty. Rumor had it that he had left Pennsylvania two jumps ahead of the law and it was the gambling interests in Sidney that had swung the election his way. Although no longer sheriff, Con McCarty was still around in March of 1880, and figured in the gold robbery on March 10.

The big gold shipment from the Black Hills came into Sidney March 9 on the stagecoach, called 'Old Ironsides' after the half-inch boiler plate lining the inside of the coach. A couple of armed men inside Old Ironsides could frustrate a gang of would-be robbers.

The stage rolled into Sidney without a hitch. Scott Davis was riding shotgun and he had a couple of his men inside the coach. Only a foolhardy highwayman would tackle that setup. Davis reported to the station agent, Chet Allen, to get the gold transferred to the train. There were over four hundred pounds of gold in bricks plus a thousand dollars in currency. The value reported varied from $119 thousand to $125 thousand. A hundred years later that much gold would be worth over $2½ million.

Here Davis ran into trouble. The train was due in an hour and Allen said it was too late to get the gold aboard. Davis argued but to no avail. The gold was stored for the night and Davis put his two men, Boon May and Gale Hill, on guard with himself. The gold got through the night safely and was brought out the next morning and transferred ready for shipment.

Davis ran into another snag. The train was due just after noon and the gold was ready before noon. Chet Allen, the station agent, had the gold on a baggage cart. Davis in-

Deadwood Stage

Courtesy Nebraska State Historical Society
Sidney, circa 1879

sisted it be put back in the safe while everyone went to dinner. But Allen said it would be perfectly safe in the station with the doors locked.

A light snow had fallen the night before and Davis tracked through it to the hotel for dinner. As he came out, someone shouted there had been a robbery at the depot. Davis dashed to the freight room where the gold had been left. Chet Allen was sitting in a chair next to the empty cart, moaning that he was ruined.

Davis saw the square hole in the floor of the baggage room big enough for a man to crawl through. Con McCarty, the ex-sheriff, was there and started yelling for a posse to look for wagon tracks. They'd be easy to follow in the snow. Four of those gold bars weighed a hundred pounds each. The thieves had to have a wagon to take it away.

That made sense except Davis didn't see any wagon tracks near the depot. He refused to go with the posse. Calling his men, he began searching. The gold obviously had been taken out through that hole in the floor. Examining the depot from the outside, he saw that it was built on stilts so that the floor was on a level with the station platform. Lat-

tice work fenced in the gap between the floor of the building and the ground.

Davis pulled away some of the lattice work and crawled under the building. Coal for winter fuel was stored under one end. He quickly saw how the hole had been cut in the floor. A bit had been used to bore almost through the floor. Dozens of holes had been bored, marking out the square. A stolen jack had been propped under that weakened spot to hold it up. Once everyone was gone from the depot, it would take only a couple of minutes to chisel out the square.

Snow had sifted in through the lattice work and Davis looked at the footprints leading from the hole in the floor to the pile of coal. Enlisting his men, they dug into the pile of coal. Underneath, they found the heavy bricks of gold. They moved them out and back up through the hole in the floor.

Davis was in the baggage room when Con McCarty and Chet Allen came back. He saw the surprise on their faces. Allen almost cried with relief at the sight. Allen had a good reputation but Davis wondered whether he was involved in the robbery.

He looked with more suspicion on Con McCarty. Two small bricks of gold were missing along with the currency. A man with a bulky coat could walk away with the small bricks in his pockets. McCarty was wearing a chinchilla coat that had huge pockets.

Davis got the four big bricks of gold tagged and loaded on the next train east. But eleven to thirteen thousand dollars in gold and currency were missing. The criminals were also missing.

The railroad sent detectives to Sidney to try to ferret out the thieves. One was James L. Smith, alias 'Whispering Smith'. He spoke softly and was a fairly pleasant appearing man, but one who placed no value on human life. Many branded him a killer.

Davis told Smith of his suspicions of McCarty and Smith quietly began his investigation. He had Chet Allen arrested. Allen later would be acquitted, mostly owing to his fine reputation.

Smith worked on the theory that McCarty was part of the ring of thieves. He soon tied Dennis Flannigan, a professional gambler, and Patrick 'Patsy' Walters, a barber, in with McCarty.

Smith could find no concrete evidence to convict any of the three men, though, so when the other detective went back to headquarters, Smith stayed to mete out his own brand of justice.

Near the end of May he marched into the Capitol Saloon where he'd seen Patsy Walters go. Moving close to Walters, Smith whispered an insult intended to be fighting words. Walters went for his gun but Smith was much faster. His first shot hit Walters in the abdomen. Walters fired wildly and his third shot hit Smith in the hand and arm. Walters went down and Smith ran to the room of Scott Davis who happened to be in town that evening. There were those in town who would gladly have lynched Smith for shooting the town barber, but Smith was arrested and lodged in jail.

Walters was badly wounded but he began to recover so Smith was charged only with attempted murder. His bail was posted by the Union Pacific. Smith kept out of sight until his hand and arm healed. It was on the last day of 1880 that Smith located Flannigan at the Lockwood House.

There had been bad blood between the two and now they didn't stop to argue. Reports said that Flannigan fired twice at Smith before Smith got his gun in his hand. Smith then fired three times. His aim was accurate twice.

Smith was charged with second-degree murder but his bail was set low and again Union Pacific agents bailed him out. Flannigan was buried on Sidney's Boot Hill.

The Union Pacific people were furious over the problems they'd had at Sidney. They warned Sidney to clean up the town or they would move their section headquarters elsewhere. The vigilantes responded to that threat.

The 'Regulators,' as they called themselves, posted notices for all undesirables to get out of town. When they didn't heed the warning, the vigilantes raided the rough element of town on the night of April 1. Rounded up with the riffraff were Con McCarty and Patsy Walters, almost recuperated from his fight with Whispering Smith. All were thrown in jail.

Two nights later a mob stormed the jail and dragged out a man named John MacDonald, one of the men picked up in the raid. MacDonald didn't have a bad reputation like some of the others and why he was singled out is uncertain. They hanged him from a telegraph pole. Some historians believe MacDonald's hanging on April 3, 1881, was the last lynching in Sidney's history.

The vigilantes took the rest of the men they had rounded up, including the ex-sheriff, Con McCarty, and Patsy Walters, and gave them a whipping at the edge of town. They sent them off threatening they'd be hanged if they came back. None did.

The soldiers and civilians of Sidney often clashed but one such clash was different from the saloon brawls. An ex-soldier named Ricketts was very fond of the military. His stepdaughter, Mary, was being courted by a soldier named Brickenbecker and a young lawyer named Henry St. Rayner. Being a military man himself, Ricketts was pressing hard for his stepdaughter to marry Brickenbecker. Mary had a mind of her own, however, and that mind was centered on St. Rayner.

The impasse was broken when Mary and Henry St. Rayner were married without the blessing of her stepfather. That should have ended the battle but to the old soldier, the battle had just begun.

One day shortly after the wedding when St. Rayner was away from home, Mary's stepfather and Brickenbecker appeared at her door. Without ceremony, they grabbed her and carted her off to the railroad depot.

At the depot, Ricketts put his stepdaughter and Brickenbecker on the train with tickets to Cheyenne. To him, that seemed the way to solve the problem.

But just before the train pulled out, St. Rayner arrived home and discovered his wife missing. Guessing his stepfather-in-law had

something to do with her disappearance, he started looking for Ricketts. Seeing him on the platform of the depot, he ran that way. Ricketts went to meet him and keep him away until the train pulled out.

The two argued but it was a short argument. The train was ready to leave. Henry had no intention of letting it get away with his wife on it.

When Ricketts, gun in hand, stood firmly in Henry's way, words gave way to guns and St. Rayner shot Ricketts. He didn't even wait to see whether he had killed him. Leaping forward, he bounded across the platform and onto the train, expecting to find Brickenbecker with a gun waiting for him. But Mary was alone. Brickenbecker apparently had no stomach for a gun battle and when he heard the shot outside, he leaped off the train on the other side.

Henry took his wife home and waited for them to come and arrest him, which they did. At his trial, however, the killing was declared self-defense and Henry went ahead

Union Pacific Depot in Sidney

Homestead shanty on the claim

with his law practice. The end of his story, however, was not that they lived happily ever after. Not long afterward, Mary died and Henry was left alone again.

The record shows that by 1882, there were over 200 burials in Sidney's cemetery. For a town so small and so young, that was a lot of deaths but few of them were from natural causes. Indians, drunken brawls, and lynchings accounted for most of them.

Many hangings occurred at Sidney but according to one old-timer, the first legal hanging came in 1885. That year, James and A. J. Pinkston, father and son, settled on land they had taken not far from Sidney. They hired a man named Reynolds to help them build a log house. They lived in a tent and cooked and ate in front of it.

On the evening of September 16, a discussion about Reynolds' wages came up. Reynolds claimed the Pinkstons owed him twelve dollars; the landowners said they owed him only seven dollars. Five dollars was hardly grounds for murder but it became just that. Reynolds killed both Pinkston men.

When the law caught up with Reynolds, he told a wild story about a man coming along and getting into a fight with the Pinkstons, killing them and forcing Reynolds to bury them. The sheriff didn't accept that. Reynolds later told what really happened.

Reynolds was tried, convicted, and sentenced to hang. According to the report, he was the first man to be legally hanged in Sidney.

Sidney had come of age.

Chapter 8

Crawford

The *Crawford Clipper* in the summer of 1980 stated: "Crawford at one time was widely known as one of the wildest towns in the West."

Crawford came into being at the very edge of a hot spot of trouble that preceded it by twelve years. Fort Robinson had been established in 1874 and when Crawford began its existence on the edge of the military reservation in 1886, it was inviting trouble. It got it.

Like most towns just outside the military reservation of a frontier fort, it was there to supply the soldiers with entertainment and vices they couldn't get on the post.

Fort Robinson, originally called Camp Red Cloud Agency, then Camp Robinson, was started out of necessity. In 1873, the Red Cloud Agency was moved from the North Platte River, near present-day Henry, north to the White River. The Indians resented being moved away from the Platte River Valley. Their resentment spewed over like a boiling pot in February of 1874.

A war party shot up the half-completed agency building, breaking every window. A teamster bringing freight to the agency was killed on the Niobrara. Then, while Dr. J. J. Savile, the Indian agent, was away, they killed the acting agent, Frank Appleton.

That triggered a quick reaction from the army and 950 soldiers were sent from Fort Laramie to the Red Cloud Agency in the bit-

Courtesy Nebraska State Historical Society

Red Cloud Agency, 1876. Trader establishment and corner of agency building.

ter cold of March to keep the peace. They camped close to the agency for a while but soon moved over to Soldier Creek and began building quarters. It was apparent that the trouble was not going to subside soon.

When gold was discovered in the Black Hills, Camp Robinson supplied the soldiers to try to keep the determined gold seekers out of the Hills which belonged to the Indians by treaty.

Doc Middleton, a name synonymous with one-way horse trading, loved Indian ponies and appropriated many from the Red Cloud Agency when the Indians and the soldiers were not looking. Perhaps it was the absence of most of the soldiers that encouraged the bravery of Middleton and his gang.

Middleton's range in Nebraska covered the entire northern half of the state and went as far south as North Platte and Sidney. Doc loved the profits he made on horse dealings—since he paid nothing for the horses except an exhibition of skill in thievery, his profits were very high. After several successful small raids on Indian pony herds near Red Cloud Agency, Doc and three cronies decided on a big raid. Doc was sure he could sell the horses at ranches north of North Platte. He'd done it before.

Doc and three companions headed for the Red Cloud Agency, determined to make a big haul. Doc and two of his men carried Winchester rifles; the fourth man had what was called a Long Tom needle gun. Near the agency they found an Indian camp with a big herd of ponies. This was it, they decided.

The Indians, however, had several guards posted around the herd. Even though they were close to Camp Robinson, they were taking no chances. The four thieves found a height from which they could watch the camp and the horse herd. They waited impatiently for the Indians to relax their guard but that time didn't come.

The thieves were running out of food and there was always the danger of being discovered by the Indians. Doc was on lookout duty when he saw a half-dozen fresh guards coming out to watch the herd. He knew there would be no chance to get that herd. Out of pure frustration, he emptied his Winchester into the Indian camp.

Predictably, the Indians swarmed out of camp like ants in a kicked-over ant hill. Doc and his companions had only one choice. That was to ride and ride fast.

It was almost night so, to be safe, they had only to keep ahead till darkness fell. The man with the needle gun experienced the misfortune of having his horse step into a hole and going down in a somersault. Neither horse nor rider was hurt but the rifle

Courtesy Nebraska State Historical Society
Soldier Buttes, Fort Robinson, Dawes County.

had been thrown quite a distance. As soon as he scrambled to his feet, he retrieved the rifle and mounted again. Then he was off toward his companions.

It was much later when the four felt they had successfully escaped pursuit. When they stopped to rest their horses the man discovered that the barrel of his needle gun was bent out of shape. He'd been carefully carrying a useless piece of junk. They'd had a narrow escape. They decided it was safer to strike at small parties than large camps and gave up any notion of stealing a big herd.

Camp Robinson became Fort Robinson in January of 1878 and just a year later took part in one of the most bizarre escapes in frontier fort history. Dull Knife and his Cheyennes had been taken to Fort Reno in Indian Territory in the fall of 1877 where they died like poisoned rats in a climate to which they were unaccustomed. They had broken out in September of 1878, leaving a path of death and destruction as they raced north, outwitting the army in every encounter until they were captured in the sandhills to the southeast of Fort Robinson.

Imprisoned at the fort and told they would have to go back to Indian Territory, they swore they would stay in their homeland or die. Food and water were withheld until they agreed to the move. On January 9, 1879, they made their break. In the snow, soldiers in underwear and bare feet tried to stop them. Many Indians and some soldiers were killed.

The chase lasted for twelve days before the last of the Indians were either killed or brought back to the fort. Dull Knife himself escaped, apparently to Canada.

Some soldiers from Fort Robinson were stationed at Camp Sheridan, some distance to the east but responsible to the commander at the fort. On Saturday night, September 20, 1880, Camp Sheridan put in its bid for some recognition as a wild spot. The report coming to Fort Robinson explained that at a "low den of iniquity" near the camp, there was a "horrible carnival of blood" that left two men dead, two seriously wounded, probably fatally, and several badly bruised.

It began when a drunken Mexican thought the bartender had swindled him and he pulled a revolver, threatening to shoot the drink dispenser. A dozen cowboys present drew their revolvers. One of them, a man named Ed Collins, was either inept at handling a gun or too drunk to control his skills. While lifting his gun from the holster, he somehow managed to shoot himself and died on the spot. The body was removed and the dance resumed within minutes.

Then a man named Jim Joyce and a roughneck cowboy named Page got into a fight over a girl known only as Beaver Tooth Nell. That ended in Page's shooting Joyce, killing him. Sergeant Green of Company M, Fifth Cavalry, was present and attempted to disarm Page. Green was shot in the leg during the struggle. Sometime later that wound necessitated the amputation of his leg. The report gave the pessimistic opinion that he would probably die from the wound.

At that moment, the seriousness of his wound was not of prime concern to the men at the dance. The soldiers present took the shooting as a personal challenge and began firing at the cowboys as they rushed to leave the building. According to the report, "The women, scantily dressed, returned from the rooms to which they had withdrawn, and ran screaming about the place, and the scene that followed baffles description."

The soldiers and the cowboys got into a free-for-all—only the arrival of a military detail from the post stopped it, probably preventing more fatalities. As it was, two were dead, one woman had an eye knocked out and two cowboys were seriously wounded. Page, who had shot Joyce, was taken to the guard house and put under heavy guard because the soldiers were threatening to lynch him. He escaped lynching and there seems to be no record of what the law did to him.

Niobrara Transportation Company's freighting train at Fort Robinson.

Fort Robinson was a main stop on the Sidney-Deadwood stage route. The stage line itself made some of the news. It was wild country through which it ran.

In early 1882, at Running Water Ranch, a station on the Sidney-Deadwood Trail, not far south of Fort Robinson, a man who had been in trouble at Fort Robinson a couple of months earlier attempted a take-over.

John Lewis had killed a cowboy at Fort Robinson in late 1881 but managed somehow to be acquitted. Later in the winter, he was at Running Water Ranch and decided he wanted to manage the ranch himself. Mrs. Hughes, who was in charge of the station attempted to drive Lewis off. Lewis pulled his gun and shot her "in the posterior." Then he fled. The cowboys at the ranch quickly formed a posse and went after him with every intention of dangling his carcass from a tree limb—if they could find a tree. No report was made as to whether they found Lewis or whether he made his escape to parts unknown. Such an insult to a lady deserved stronger punishment than banishment from the area, the cowboys felt.

A town rising in such an environment was almost predestined to be wild. Crawford fulfilled its potential. The fort had struggled along for twelve years without a town near it where the soldiers could blow off steam. In 1886, the Fremont, Elkhorn & Missouri Valley Railroad built across northern Nebraska from the northeastern corner of the state all the way into Wyoming. It reached Fort Robinson that year and almost immediately a town began bulging out of the prairie.

The town was situated right on the edge of the military reservation, typical of most fort towns. Inside the reservation, even if the military had allowed it, the town would have been subject to military rule. Outside, only the men who wanted to reap a financial harvest made the rules.

Just three years before the railroad came, William Edwards Annon, a son-in-law of Joseph W. Paddock and brother-in-law of Benjamin Paddock, the post sutler, arrived at Fort Robinson to write some feature sto-

The first house in Dawes County

Post Sutler's Store at Fort Robinson.

ries about the fort and its army life for the Omaha Bee newspaper. He took a tree claim at the northeastern cormer of the military reservation. When the railroad came through, it cut through the heart of the tree claim. Annon sold his land for the townsite and made a very handsome profit.

The town took its name from Captain Emmet Crawford, who had been at Camp Robinson it its early days as a lieutenant. He had been killed while chasing Apaches in Mexico in January of 1886.

A temporary inhabitant of Crawford when it began to mushroom was Calamity Jane Canary. She lived in a tent, as many of the first residents did, in the north side of town. On this trip, and perhaps on other trips to the vicinity of Fort Robinson, she brought a wagon with cooking equipment. Her mission was to recruit dancing girls for the saloons in Deadwood. She had little trouble finding them. Crawford in its early days was seldom short of this commodity.

On two different occasions, Negro troops were stationed at Fort Robinson. The Ninth Cavalry, a black unit, was at the fort from

Algernon S. Paddock, Brother of J. W. Paddock and Uncle of Ben Paddock, Post Sutler at Fort Robinson.

Second and Elm Streets, southeast corner, Crawford, May 1886

Black soldiers on horses, Fort Robinson, 1889

1885 until it was called to war duty in 1898. There supposedly were no racial problems but often trouble erupted among the blacks themselves and between them and the white soldiers. This trouble was not always confined to the fort. Crawford drew its portion.

First Sergeant Emmanuel Stance was a black soldier in the Ninth Cavalry. He had more than his share of trouble with his men. This trouble could not be attributed to racial problems for they were all black. Army reports show that soldiers accused the sergeant of an overbearing attitude beyond the authority of a sergeant. These complaints might well have been forgotten if he had not been found dead on Christmas Day, 1887, draped over a fence between Crawford and Fort Robinson. It was obviously murder but the killer was not ascertained. Most suspi-

cion was directed at his own men, the soldiers of F Troop. He was given a military funeral and buried in the post cemetery but records do not indicate anything further was done. Conditions being what they were, each man had to take care of himself.

One of the army's best scouts at Fort Robinson was Baptiste Garnier. Everyone called him "Little Bat." He had a brother, also a scout, who was called "Big Bat." Their father was French and their mother Sioux. Little Bat had a hand in trying to smooth over the difficulties that arose with the Ghost Dance. At that time in 1890, he was the post

Baptiste Garnier "Little Bat," (lower right), Jack Red Cloud (son of Chief Red Cloud), Chief Red Cloud, Chief Knife.

Ninth or Tenth Troops Cavalry, Fort Robinson, 1889

scout at Fort Robinson. He was of the opinion that the Ghost Dance would die of its own accord if the white men would just stand back and let it run its course. But the white men were still jittery over the possibility of more Indian trouble and, as usual, could not stand back.

That all ended in the battle of Wounded Knee in late December, 1890, with heavy losses to big Foot's band of Indians, and several casualties among the troopers of the Seventh Cavalry. Little Bat was there as interpreter and was helping disarm the Indians when the battle began. Half-white, half-Indian, he was torn between two cultures. It would lead to fatal consequences for Little Bat in years to come.

Perhaps Crawford's chief claim to fame was its proximity to Fort Robinson. The county seat was at Chadron, twenty miles to the northeast. Crawford tried to take care of its own troubles and did not often call on the county sheriff. For some time the county had a good sheriff who was to become better known later as the mayor of Omaha. James Dahlman used strategy to work his way out of tight spots.

One of those tight spots came as the result of an incident in a rural area some distance from Crawford. Warren Shistler lived on land well away from a creek where most of the earliest settlers had taken land. He had dug a well. In order to work in the well as it was dug, the hole had to be at least three feet in diameter.

The Shistlers had suffered the misfortune of losing all four of their children in an epidemic of diphtheria. After burying their children, they adopted a boy. This boy and his adopted mother were alone on the homestead one day when a man wandered into the yard. Mrs. Shistler did not know him but he wanted a drink from the well. This was not unusual—all strangers were invited to get water for themselves and their horses.

This stranger, however, seemed to have trouble getting the water and asked for help. Mrs. Shistler went to the well to show him how to draw water, although it seemed unbelievable that he didn't know how to perform that simple task.

When Mrs. Shistler reached the well, the stranger suddenly shoved her into the hole. She grabbed at the curbing and got a good grip with one hand. The stranger kicked her fingers loose and she dropped to a ledge well down inside the well. There was no logical reason for the act.

The adopted son was close enough to see what had happened and he came to the well crying as the stranger rode off. He was still there sobbing when men from the Half Diamond E ranch happened by. They investigated and found Mrs. Shistler on the ledge. In a short time, they had her out of the well.

The boy was able to point the direction the stranger had gone. They immediately took out after the man. They caught up with him and took him to Chadron where Sheriff Dahlman put him in jail.

Word of the event spread like a prairie fire through the town and talk of lynching spread as fast as the story. It was after noon. Sheriff Dahlman understood the situation; he was sure that as soon as darkness came, the mob would materialize. Sensing he might not be able to control the mob, he called a deputy and sent him out to the edge of town to start a ball game. Everyone loved a ball game and the deputy had no trouble finding enough men for two teams. By the time the game started, three-fourths of the town was out to watch.

While the game was going on, Dahlman got the prisoner out of the jail and hurried him off to Rushville, county seat of Sheridan County, thirty miles to the east. There he was turned over to the sheriff of that county and officers took him right on to Lincoln where there would be no danger of lynching. The man was tried in Lincoln, convicted and put into the penitentiary. Credit for avoiding a lynching which would have given Chadron and Dawes County a black mark went to Sheriff Dahlman.

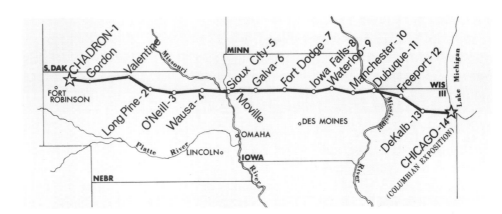

*Courtesy Nebraska State
Historical Society*

Map of the Chadron–Chicago
cowboy race in 1893.

When the drought of the early '90s came, Jim Dahlman was instrumental in creating some excitement and business for Dawes County by getting into a hundred-mile horse race. Dahlman himself did not ride but he entered the horse that won the race. This race fostered the thousand-mile race from Chadron to Chicago, making the headlines over all the country.

The race started early on June 13, 1893, and the winner, John Berry, arrived at Buffalo Bill's Wild West Show in Chicago one thousand and forty miles and thirteen days and sixteen hours later. During that month of June, Chadron and Dawes County were in the news far and wide. *John Berry was disqualified as he had helped plan the route, 2nd winner disqualified as he had put his horses on the train part of the way. Gillespie was given a gun. His family gave it to the Dawes County Historical museum.*

*Courtesy Nebraska State
Historical Society*

Gillespie and Smith, two participants in the Chadron–Chicago horse race, 1893.

Two years later Crawford was the scene of a quarrel over some hay. The quarrel escalated to murder. Arthur Morrison was city marshal of Crawford but his position as law officer had nothing to do with the trouble. It started innocently enough in the fall of 1894 when a man named McManus contracted with C. Y. Akes and Byron Jackson to cut and put up two hundred tons of hay.

The trouble started when Jackson demanded money the two men had earned and McManus said he had already paid them in full. Jackson and Akes said they would sell the hay to get their money if necessary. McManus had already sold a half interest in the hay to Marshal Arthur Morrison. The hay

was still in the field, baled and ready to haul out.

Morrison and McManus went out to get the hay. Akes tried to stop them but Morrison had his rifle and stood guard while the hay was loaded and hauled to his barn in Crawford. Then Morrison arrested Jackson for trying to sell hay that was not his.

On the day of Jackson's trial, January 17, 1895, a new element was thrust on the scene. Addison Von Harris, a respected man in Crawford, was defending Byron Jackson at the trial. That morning Harris brought an officer to Morrison's barn to take charge of the hay stored there. He had an order saying a man named Albert Whipple owned the hay. Likely, Jackson had sold some of the hay to Whipple.

Morrison had his barn locked and swore he'd shoot anybody who attempted to break the lock. Harris and Morrison exchanged hot words. Harris was a big man, weighing about two hundred and twenty pounds. Morrison was a heavyset man, short, weighing about one hundred and eighty pounds. Morrison sent for his Winchester and promised Harris there would be some shooting if any more attempts were made to get his hay. What Harris said in reply is lost to history.

The trial went on as scheduled and it was late in the afternoon when Morrison charged into the courtroom. Spotting Harris, he made for him, revolver in hand. Stopping in front of Harris, he accused him of planning to burn his barn. Harris denied it vehemently.

Morrison tried to gun whip Harris but Harris grabbed his hand, wrapped his other arm around Morrison's neck and choked him down. Friends of both men leaped in to stop the fight. Morrison's gun went off, the bullet hitting a man named Lyons in the shoulder. Then the two men were pulled apart.

Marshal Morrison went out the back door, shouting at Harris, "I'll fix you." Harris apparently paid little attention to the threat. He went outside, the trial having been disrupted by the uproar.

Five minutes later Morrison found Harris there talking to some friends. No words were spoken. Morrison shot him with his Winchester, the bullet apparently going through his neck, probably killing him instantly.

The people on the street seemed stunned as Morrison turned and ran back down the street. Addison Von Harris never carried a gun and was not armed when he was killed. Some reports said afterward that someone had shot at Morrison before he killed Harris. Most people said only one shot was fired, the one that killed Harris. If there was another shot, speculation was that C. Y. Akes had fired it. However, to most people, it was a case of outright murder.

Morrison escaped from town while the coroner was called from Chadron. His investigation could lead to only one conclusion but the townsfolk wanted it official. Men in Crawford were eager to form a posse and go after Morrison but Morrison, being a lawman himself, realized his best chances of survival were under the protection of the law. He sent word to the sheriff in Chadron that he was willing to give himself up and before the night was over, he was escorted into the jail at Chadron.

On Sunday, January 20, Harris's funeral was held in Crawford. Over five hundred people crowded into the firemen's hall or stood just outside for the service. It would have been an ordinary funeral for a favorite man except for the unexpected ending.

Courtesy Nebraska State Historical Society
Settler's home near Crawford, Dawes County. Crow Butte is at the right.

After those attending had viewed the body, the father of the murdered man moved up to the casket and in a loud voice called upon God to avenge the murder of his son.

Morrison's trial was held in county court. One juror stated that if he had his way, Morrison would hang. Because of that, Morrison got a new trial and a change of venue. The second trial was held in Rushville, county seat of Sheridan County. Here he was acquitted, to the disgust of those who had witnessed the murder.

On the tombstone of Addison Von Harris in the cemetery a couple of miles north of Crawford, these words are chiseled:

Assassinated on the streets of Crawford, Nebraska, Jan. 17, 1895, age 38 years, 2 months, 6 days. I am the resurrection and the life. He that believeth in me shall never die. When they who shield the assassin's hand and share the awful crime with him stand before the bar of God, in His truth will right the wrong and sin.

Photo by the author

Tombstone of Addison Von Harris in Crawford cemetery. He was killed by Arthur Morrison in January 1895.

The year 1898 saw many of the soldiers at Fort Robinson shipped off to fight in Cuba. The 9th Cavalry unit was sent so there were no Negro soldiers at the fort for a while.

Baptiste Garnier, or "Little Bat," the army scout, was well respected around the fort and Crawford, even though he was half Sioux. On Saturday evening, December 15, 1900, Little Bat and some friends went into George Dietrich's Saloon on the corner of 2nd and Main in Crawford and ordered some drinks. Jim Haguewood was bartender. Apparently some bad blood flowed between him and Little Bat. Perhaps it was simply that Little Bat was half Indian. Indians occupied the lowest social level in the area at that time.

Haguewood demanded payment for the drinks from Little Bat, practically accusing him of trying to steal the drinks. Little Bat had a reputation for being absolutely honest. He reached into his pocket—those around him said it was for the little pouch in which he kept his money. Haguewood afterward swore he was reaching for his gun.

Haguewood wheeled around and grabbed the gun he always kept handy and shot Little Bat. The scout was knocked almost off his feet—he turned and staggered toward the door. Haguewood shot him again in the back. Little Bat got through the door and out into the street where he staggered part way across to the opposite corner and collapsed.

Dr. Meredith was called and Little Bat was taken inside where the doctor could tend him. The scout died a little after three o'clock on Sunday morning, December 16.

Jim Haguewood was brought to trial for the killing. The jury deliberated over two days and nights before reaching a verdict of, "not guilty". The 'doubt' in the mind of jury was whether Haguewood really thought Little Bat was reaching for his gun. One of the jurors who finally had to cross over to the 'not guilty' verdict was still not convinced after the trial. He believed Haguewood had only been looking for an excuse to kill Little Bat.

Courtesy Nebraska State Historical Society
Baptiste Garnier and family at Fort Robinson.

Some thought the 'not guilty' verdict resulted from the general feeling of the citizens in the area toward the Indians. After all, Little Bat was part Indian (to many that made him all Indian) and he had been killed by a white man. That in itself made it almost guilt-free.

Little Bat, as Chief of Scouts, was laid to rest in the Fort cemetery. Perhaps his stone implies a great deal about his status: it simply said, "Employee."

In early May of 1902, the 10th Cavalry came to Fort Robinson. These were the first black soldiers since the 9th Cavalry left for Cuba in 1898. There were three hundred and fifty-eight men plus nine officers in the 10th, along with four hundred horses. The people of Crawford would have told a reporter quickly there was no racial prejudice in their town. Perhaps that would have been true initially, but trouble erupted later between the blacks and whites.

Horse racing was a big thing both at the fort and in the town. An incident occurred at one of these races at the fort that has been handed down by word of mouth. It likely would have been forgotten had it not been for events that took place a year later.

In this particular race on July 4, 1905, the town marshal, Arthur Moss, entered his horse. Several soldiers also entered the race. The one involved in the incident was a sergeant in the 10th Cavalry, a black man named John Reid.

It was not a long race, following the track around a lagoon. Most races tested the horses in their ability to get away from the post fast and to maintain an all-out speed for the distance. As the horses neared the finish line, two were well out in front. One was ridden by the black soldier, John Reid, and the other by the town marshal, Arthur Moss. According to the report, the two horses were neck and neck until the marshal, who was whipping his horse with a quirt, reached over and slapped the other rider, causing him to

Courtesy Nebraska State Historical Society
First 4th of July celebration in Crawford

Bad blood between the two survived through the winter.   On Sunday May 13, 1906 – nice day for a picnic,   A group of black soldiers bought several kegs of beer & proceeded to have a grand time.. By 7:30 in the evening they were abusively boisterous.   Marshal Moss ordered them to quiet down & disperse.

Most left except for a group of five. John Reid was one of them; They had a fight. The Marshall died from a gun shot.

Reid & another black man

two black men ran to a home of Mrs Edna Ewing, an old colored lady. Joe Hand saw them run pass his place & go into Mrs Ewing home. He notified people & they began to gather around her home.   The one man panicked, broke out of the house & ran toward the Fort. Some of the men in the crowd shot him. Before he died he told them Reid was hiding in the attic.   Reid was put in the local jail until he was transferred to the county jail in Chadron by train that evening.

& Army guards.

All officers were on alert for either a lynch mob or a rescue party. They did get him to the county jail – Never told what happened to Reid.

jerk away, thus throwing his horse off stride, and losing the race. Arthur Moss declared Reid had reached over and grabbed the bridle of his horse and that he had struck back in self-defense. *see paper*.

Moss, feeling elated over his victory, was encouraged to punish the man who, he insisted, had almost cost him the race. The report says he rode his horse over to a cluster of Negroes which included Reid, and clubbed Reid over the head a couple of times with his quirt. Another man was with Moss; he dispersed the group quickly. Whether the reporter recalled the incident exactly as it happened or not, the bad blood between the two apparently survived through the winter and was still virulent the next summer.

On Sunday, May 13, 1906—a nice enough day for a picnic—a group of black soldiers bought several kegs of beer and proceeded to have a grand time. By 7:30 in the evening, they were drunk enough to become abusively boisterous. Marshal Arthur Moss

was called to quiet them. He went to the west end of Linn Street where the black soldiers were creating the disturbance and ordered them to quiet down and disperse.

Most of the soldiers left the scene as ordered but a few remained in a little knot, defying the marshal. In the center of this group of five was John Reid, the man Ross had tangled with at the 4th of July horse race the previous summer. Close to Reid was a friend, Jordan Taylor. With the marshal was his brother, Jim H. Moss, and a friend, Wren Gering.

Moss approached this group, demanding they disperse and leave town. Jim Moss warned his brother that Reid had a gun in his hand, hiding it between his side and the fence where he was standing. Arthur Moss was gripping his gun and he pointed it at Reid, yelling for him to drop his gun. Reid started to obey but then changed his mind. Reports vary as to who fired the first shot.

Jim Moss leaped forward and grabbed

Courtesy Nebraska State Historical Society

Soldiers on horses parading in Crawford.

Reid's arm and tried to wrest the gun from him. Reid turned his attention to J. H. Moss for a moment. Then his friend, Jordan Taylor, swung a club at Jim's head. It missed his head but struck him on the arm, temporarily paralyzing it. Jim was out of the fight. The marshal was down, shot in the side. He died shortly afterward. It was never determined whether it was Reid's first or later shots that did the damage. Many thought it must have been the first shot or Marshal Moss would have shot Reid during his struggle with Jim Moss.

With the marshal dying and Jim Moss incapacitated by the blow to his arm, Reid and Taylor turned and ran toward some homes nearby. Wren Gering leaped forward and grabbed Arthur Moss's gun. He fired several shots at the two fleeing soldiers but apparently his aim was poor.

The black men ran to the home of Mrs. Edna Ewing, an old colored lady, and she hid them. They might have escaped detection if a man named Joe Hand had not seen them running past his place and followed them. He made sure they had gone into Mrs. Ewing's house and then he sent word to authorities while he stood guard a short distance away to make certain the two didn't leave the Ewing house.

People began to gather like bees around a bunch of clover. Jordan Taylor panicked when he realized their hiding place had been located. He broke out of the house, running wildly toward the fort three miles away. The crowd surged after him, yelling for him to halt. He only ran harder. Some of the men in the crowd stopped and fired several shots at him. Some hit the soldier and he went down. Before he died, he told those who caught up with him that Reid was hiding in the attic of Mrs. Ewing's house.

The crowd surged back to the Ewing house and the authorities went inside, cautiously searching the house. They found Reid cringing in the attic above the kitchen. He was disarmed and taken to Judge Heywood for preliminary hearing. Then he was lodged in the local jail until he was transferred to Chadron to the county jail on the train that evening.

However, word came that the train was running five hours late. That presented problems. The authorities were deluged with rumors. They heard that friends of Marshal Arthur Moss were assembling a lynch mob to take Reid out and hang him to make sure

Photo by author
Tombstone of Marshal Arthur Moss in Crawford cemetery. He was killed by John Reid in May 1906.

he paid for his crime. Other rumors said that members of B Troop, Reid's outfit at the fort, were planning a rescue attempt.

Those in charge of Reid weighed the likelihood of some of the rumors' being true and decided they had to deliver Reid to Chadron quickly. They couldn't wait for the train. So they made plans to get a team and wagon and slip it up to the little town jail and take Reid to Chadron in the wagon.

With all officers on the alert for either a lynch mob or a rescue party, the evacuation plans were almost complete when a detachment of soldiers arrived from the fort. They brought both disquieting and reassuring news.

A check of rifles and ammunition at the fort revealed that Troop B, Reid's Company, had several rifles and a quantity of ammunition missing. Also several members of Troop B were unaccounted for. The officers were convinced that a rescue attempt was under way. The troops, sent to town by Colonel Augur, had orders to help guard the prisoner and maintain order. The authorities welcomed them and quickly changed their plans. With troops on guard around the jail, they could afford to wait for the tardy train.

Just having the troops in place around the jail did not eliminate the possibility of trouble, however. They all knew that and it increased the tension. The saloons in town were doing a booming business. In Bruer's Saloon, a man named Phil Murphy, likely the worse for having imbibed too much of the house's merchandise, demanded the loan of a gun. He said he wanted to shoot someone. He was turned down, of course. He wheeled on the bartender with some abusive language that was not well received. The bartender grabbed Murphy and literally threw him out of the saloon, not even taking time to open the door first. Murphy's head slammed into the glass in the door, shattering it.

Murphy wasn't badly hurt and he went on a rampage, finally heading for the jail. He ran past the first soldier who was standing guard. The soldier called for him to halt but he went on past the second sentry. That soldier, Private Stephen Collier of I Company, 10th Cavalry, called twice for him to halt but he ignored him as he had the first sentry. Private Collier fired once, knocking Murphy off his feet. Men hurried out and carried Murphy into the jail and put him on a cot where he died a short time later.

The town settled down then until the train came in. Sheriff Mote was present by this time and took Reid to the train, accompa-

Courtesy Nebraska State Historical Society

Colonel W. H. Ketcham, 1906, near Crawford

nied by the local officers and several of the army guards. The rescue party of B Troop didn't show up at the jail. Perhaps the shooting of Phil Murphy cooled their enthusiasm for a rescue attempt.

Private Collier was exonerated of all blame for shooting Murphy since he was merely following orders. Mrs. Ewing was bound over to district court for trial in aiding the killer, John Reid. Fourteen rifles were found hidden on the boundary of the military reservation at the edge of Crawford, and seven members of B Troop who had been missing the night John Reid was in jail in Crawford were arrested and placed in the fort guardhouse.

Some laid the blame for so much violence in Crawford in the first decade of the 1900s on the fact that there was no liquor, not even beer, sold on the military reservations so the soldiers came to Crawford where they could get it. In just the few years that the 10th Cavalry was stationed at Fort Robinson, there were at least four other murders in Crawford; some were attributed to the soldiers. None created quite as much uproar, however, as that of Marshal Arthur Moss.

One murder occurred on the post. The fort photographer, C. B. Brown, who seemed to have no enemies anywhere, was found one morning in his apartment at the fort, shot through the head. It was Monday, January 21, 1907, that the alarm over the disappearance of the photographer prompted some of his friends to take action. He hadn't called for his mail and no one could recall having seen him for a couple of days. They broke the lock on his apartment and found him dead with a bullet hole in the back of his head. The hair was singed, indicating he had been shot at close range.

Investigation began at once, in hopes of finding a clue as to who had committed the crime. About all the detective work revealed was that the murderer must have been visiting Brown in the evening, judging from the way the photographer was dressed and the fact that the bullet had been fired at such close range.

Brown was buried in the military cemetery. The size of the funeral attested to his many friends. No one could think of even a single enemy of his.

Crawford, as well as its neighbor, Fort Robinson, was not the epitome of genteel civilization in the first decade of the twentieth century.

Courtesy Nebraska State Historical Society

Log barracks at Old Post, Fort Robinson, built in 1883

Chapter 9

Valentine

First came the fort, then the town. Fort Niobrara along the Niobrara River was established April 22, 1880. Its purpose was to ensure that the Indians stayed on their reservations and didn't bother the homesteaders who were beginning to settle along the river. The big Pine Ridge Reservation in South Dakota was to the northwest and the Rosebud Reservation was directly north.

Like most frontier posts, Fort Niobrara attracted camp followers. One man built a tavern not far from the post. Some called it the Deer Park Hotel.

In early May of 1881, the post blacksmith decided to spend the night at the hotel. The walls were thin and the blacksmith could hear every word from the men in the adjoining room.

The next morning he rushed back to the post commander, Major J. J. Upham, to tell him of the plans to hold up the stagecoach coming into Fort Niobrara on May 9. That coach would be bringing Colonel T. H. Stanton from headquarters at Fort Omaha with the monthly payroll. The money would be in cash because the soldiers wanted something they could spend immediately.

Major Upham decided the blacksmith was telling the truth so he sent a detachment of cavalry under the command of Lieutenant Samuel Cherry to Long Pine, the first settlement down the Niobrara River and twenty miles east of the spot where the robbers were planning to hold up the stage.

The troops met the stage there and escorted it to Fort Niobrara without incident. Some doubted there ever was a robbery plot but others thought the presence of the troops had thwarted it. Events later that evening proved the blacksmith had been right.

The men were paid and went immediately out to celebrate, heading for Casterline's Ranche, two or three miles east of the fort. Being off the military reservation, Casterline's sold liquor, provided gambling tables, room for dancing, and beds for those who preferred to spend the night there.

With their pay burning holes in their pockets, the soldiers' party waxed into a real celebration. Then about midnight, three masked men, carrying Winchester rifles, burst into the place and demanded everyone's money. Everyone froze except the bartender, Casterline himself, who dropped behind his bar. Obviously he had anticipated something like this. The masked men fired their rifles at the bar. When Casterline came up, he had a shotgun. His first shot seriously wounded one of the robbers, Dick Burr, and slightly wounded another, Private Johnson, who had abandoned his guard post at the fort to join in the holdup. The other robber, Tedde Reade, was not injured.

The blast from the shotgun seemed to bring every gun in the hall into action. Bullets flew everywhere. A half-breed Indian, Johnny Bordeaux from the Rosebud Reservation, was killed. Others were wounded. In the melee, the three holdup men escaped into the breaks along the Niobrara River.

Early the next morning the army took action. Private Johnson was AWOL and three of the best army horses and rifles were missing. Lieutenant Cherry was detailed to head a search party of eighteen men to run down the renegades.

They headed directly for the breaks along the Niobrara River in pursuit of the three outlaws' trail. They found it but then lost it.

Lieutenant Cherry divided his detail to search for it. They covered the area west as far as McCann Canyon and the Minnechaduza River. They met at the northern headquarters of Jed Sharpe's ranch and spent the night there.

Lieutenant Cherry dispatched a messenger back to the fort with a report of the day's search and a request to send more supplies to Clarke's Ranch, about fifteen miles north of the fort.

At the fort, Major Upham sent a sergeant with the supplies and also reinforcements for Lieutenant Cherry. Cherry started out from Sharpe's Ranch early on the morning of May 11, heading in the general direction of Clarke's Ranch to meet with the supplies he had ordered. He sent out scouts in several directions to check for signs of the outlaws.

Just before they came to a little stream called Rock Creek, they spotted a lone rider to the south. Cherry thought it might be one of the fugitives so he sent some men to investigate. He had only three men left with him then: Sergeant Harrington, Private Conroy and Private Thomas Locke.

They stopped at the creek and Private Locke dismounted to get a drink. As he remounted, he pulled out his pistol and shot at Private Conroy. His missed, but then wheeled and galloped toward Lieutenant Cherry and Sergeant Harrington. Getting close to Lieutenant Cherry, he jabbed the gun in his side and pulled the trigger. Cherry was dead when he fell off his horse.

Meanwhile, Locke turned his gun on Conroy again and shot him in the thigh. Conroy was knocked out of the saddle.* Locke spurred his horse to the west over the trail they had just traveled. The lone rider they

had seen turned out to be the advance scout for the reinforcements coming from Fort Niobrara.

Sergeant Harrington panicked when Cherry was shot and spurred his horse into a wild run. He showed up late that day at the fort and was placed in the guardhouse for deserting his post.

Locke spent that night back at Sharpe's north ranch and the next night at Sharpe's south ranch. From there he went southeast till he got a job on a ranch south of present-day Bassett. Someone there recognized and arrested him, though, taking him back to Fort Niobrara. From there he was quickly transported to Deadwood, South Dakota. Lieutenant Cherry had been a very well-liked man and antipathy toward Locke was high at the fort. At his trial, he was found guilty and sentenced to prison in the federal penitentiary in Michigan.

As for the three holdup men, they were apprehended as they tried to cross the Missouri River at Fort Pierre. They were jailed at Yankton, awaiting trial at Deadwood. They made a jail break. Private Johnson was killed in the attempt. Dick Burr, who had been seriously wounded by the shotgun blast at Casterline's, made good his escape. Tedde Reade was recaptured and taken to Deadwood for trial. There he was found guilty—it was also discovered that he was wanted for a previous murder. Reports state simply that he was 'executed.'

As a memorial to Lieutenant Samuel Cherry, the county, when it was organized in 1883, was named Cherry County.

In the spring of 1882, the railroad grade came through and a town sprang up on the southeast side of the Niobrara River. It was known as the 'Big Cut,' referring to the deep gash cut through the bluff for the railroad grade to reach the bridge across the river. The town was really divided, half on either side of the cut. It was as wild as most railroad construction towns were. There was a sporting house near the tracks between the

---

*After diligent research, this author never found any reason for Locke to turn on Conroy and Cherry. He must have held grudges toward the two, but the explanation is lost in history.

two sections of the town. It was here that another murder took place before either the county or the town of Valentine came into official existence.

Ida Miller, better known as 'Big Foot Ide,' was killed at the sporting house by the man who lived with her, Norris Miller. Miller left the country fast. He was never heard from again.

Some felt that Ida Miller had a premonition that something like this might happen because she had requested that she be buried at a certain spot just across the canyon from the sporting house. Her wishes were honored.

That fall of 1882, with a new town springing out of the prairie over on the north side of the Niobrara River, close to Fort Niobrara, a meeting was held at the Deer Park Hotel to give the new town a name. The name "Valentine"was chosen, honoring their Congressman from West Point, E. K. Valentine.

The railroad tracks got as far as the east side of the Niobrara River that fall of 1882.

Courtesy Nebraska State Historical Society

D. Y. Mears, the man who surveyed and named Cherry County

Courtesy Nebraska State Historical Society

Niobrara River near Valentine, Cherry County

A town was born there named Thacher for J. M. Thacher, the post trader at Fort Niobrara.

The FL outfit, with R. R. Greenland as foreman, shipped cattle east from Thacher that fall. The ranch manager went with the cattle to Chicago. He ordered his foreman to get the FL cowboys out of Thacher before nightfall because the town was not a safe place for anybody at night. It was too late, though, to get far enough away from Thacher that the cowboys wouldn't be able to return, so Greenland decided the FL would stay in town.

The cook for the crew was Andy Bartlett. He had gotten acquainted with a gambler he liked. Late that night he came to Greenland, who had bedded down beside a freight building with his gun under his head. Greenland was barely aware of which of his men had awakened him.

Later Greenland heard gunshots on the other side of the building and ran around to find Andy Bartlett dead. Bartlett had not been involved in the fight. He had come to Greenland for a gun and had slipped it away from Greenland's bed while he was talking to him. Then he had given it to the gambler so he could protect himself from another man who was claiming a lady of the night that the gambler also claimed. Somehow in the fracas, the gambler had shot Bartlett. the shooting was declared an accident.

Andy Bartlett came from Friend, Nebraska, but Greenland got no reply from a telegram he sent to Bartlett's family so the cowboy was buried there on the Niobrara.

By the summer of 1883, Valentine was a growing village. The county had officially come into being on April 4 of that spring, but Valentine wouldn't be incorporated until January 8, 1884, but it was a bustling town in '83. It had no cemetery until August of that summer. On the 31st of July word reached town that Peg Leg Jack had been killed at his road house four or five miles up the Minnechaduza River from Valentine. A cor-

oner's jury reached a verdict of suicide but many had doubts about that. There were no doubts, however, about the next move. Valentine had to have a cemetery. They laid out one on a small hill a half mile from town overlooking the Minnechaduza River and J. K. Adams, better known as Peg Leg Jack, was its first resident.

A few discreet people called a new rowdy establishment about a quarter of a mile outside town, "the dance hall south of town." Most people called it the Hog Ranche. It was the scene of a shooting on October 12, 1883 in which the prime participants were the new sheriff of Cherry County, Johnny Key, and a Wyoming cowboy from the OW ranch near Manville. The OW cowboys had shipped out some horses and were bent on having a grand time. It happened to be the same evening Sheriff Key and a friend, Sam Earnest, also decided to seek entertainment at the "dance hall."

Apparently a few Wyoming boys, particularly Clarence Hand, held a grudge against either the sheriff or Sam Earnest.

There was plenty of name calling and threatening when the two groups met at the Hog Ranche in the afternoon but the cowboys went away, promising to come back. Key assumed it was all a bluff. He and Earnest stayed at the ranch, sure they would hear no more from the OW boys.

But the Wyoming cowboys returned while Key was in a back room with one of the girls. He heard them yelling outside, threatening to ride their horses right into the bar. The bartender was begging them not to.

Key rushed out to stop the fuss but there is no mention of what happened to Earnest. He must have run just as hard, but out the back door. As Key came into the room between the stove and the bar, one of the men spotted him and yelled: "Here is Key now!" Then he punctuated his statement with a shot.

Guns erupted all along the front of the building. Key dived for cover and dug out his gun. Sizing up the situation, he realized one man had his horse halfway through the door and was almost stuck there as others tried to crowd their horses inside, too.

Key fired twice; the cowboy on the lead horse tumbled out of the saddle and rolled outside the doorway. That extinguished some of the remaining cowboys' enthusiasm. They dismounted and ran around the corner of the building, but they didn't give up the fight. They charged at the door, trying to get in and finish the job the dead cowboy had started but they were driven back by Key and the bartender.

Key didn't need the situation explained to him. He was no match for that many guns. He made for the back door and escaped, even though several shots were fired at him.

He sneaked into his room in town, slept through the night, and turned himself over to the law the next morning. The town was preparing for an all-out assault from the cowboys to get revenge for one of their number being killed. All businesses in town were closed and all the men were armed.

Key was arrested but released when the coroner's jury concluded that the killing was a clear case of self-defense.

The blame for the ruckus was never pinpointed. All fingers pointed toward Clarence Hand who held a grudge against Key, Earnest, or a man named Billy Carter. Carter was running for sheriff in that fall's elections. All agreed that it was Clarence Hand who was out to do the killing and he was the one who got killed. Hand's was the second burial in the Minnechaduza cemetery.

Early in December of that year, tragedy added still another resident to the new cemetery. Bad blood had been building up between two men who had married sisters, Mary and Lucy McDonald. J. J. Hamlin was an employee of the Wyoming Cattlemen's Association. His brother-in-law was Johnny Smith. The two men had been at odds for some time.

Two distinct versions were told of the events leading up to the murder as well as the murder itself. This is understandable since one version came from the wife of the murdered man and the other from the killer.

J. J. Hamlin came home from O'Neill on a train that happened to be carrying Johnny Smith. They had an argument and, according to one report, only intervention by the train crew prevented a killing right there.

Hamlin had recently moved from Deer Park to Valentine, where he lived on the south edge of town. Hamlin told his wife about his trouble with Smith; she insisted that he not go to Billy Carter's saloon that day as he usually did. Carter was a friend of Johnny Smith and Hamlin was liable to get into trouble there.

Shortly before noon he got his horse and headed out on the prairie south of town to look for another horse that had strayed. Johnny Smith came from town and rode out onto the prairie south of town, too. He had Billy Carter, the incoming sheriff, his deputy-to-be, Jesse Danielson, and a man named Pierce with him. The two stories of what happened vary greatly.

The Valentine Reporter printed the story Smith told them. The paper said Smith and Hamlin had agreed to meet on the south of town at noon to settle their differences, so it was a duel, not a murder. The only eye witnesses were Carter, Danielson and Pierce, and they supported Smith's story.

Hamlin's widow went to the *O'Neill Frontier* with her report, telling how her brother-in-law, Johnny Smith, had threatened Hamlin. She said her husband didn't carry a gun and had no gun with him when he was killed out on the prairie.

Whether or not anyone believed her story, an indictment was filled against the four men. Smith, perhaps feeling that his story could not stand the light of an investigation, skipped the country. He was arrested in Arizona but escaped before he could be extradited. A later report said he was killed in Mexico while resisting arrest. Carter, Danielson and Pierce were brought to trial but later acquitted.

Somewhere between the stories told by Smith in the *Reporter* and Mrs. Hamlin in the *Frontier* lies the truth. But the result of the incident was one nobody could deny. J. J. Hamlin was the next person to make a one way trip to the Minnechaduza cemetery.

As the military post grew, so did the town of Valentine. It had more saloons than stores and was rapidly acquiring a reputation as one of the roughest towns in the state. An officer from the fort came into town one day and was shocked to see the body of a man dangling from a rope tied to a telegraph pole. It was a short distance from the depot so the officer stopped there to ask the stationmaster what he knew about it.

The stationmaster informed him indignantly that somebody had had the nerve to hang the man right in front of the station the previous night. The stationmaster couldn't allow the body to be there when trains came by.

"Imagine what that would to do the reputation of Valentine!" he exclaimed.

So, with some help, he had cut the body down and moved it up a couple of poles away from the station. Valentine's good reputation had to be preserved.

The activities of the area seemed to be more than the law could or wanted to han-

dle. This resulted in the organization of a vigilance committee. Sometimes the vigilantes trod on the toes of decent citizens but they were tolerated in view of what life would be without them.

Vigilantes seemed out of place when they arrested a young man named P. J. Cline. Cline and his sixteen-year-old bride-to-be, Mary Berry, had come to town to get married. After the ceremony, when they had registered at a nice hotel, vigilantes from Holt county descended on the hotel and arrested Cline.

The vigilantes had been hot on the trail of Kid Wade's horse thieves. They claimed that Cline was a member of that gang and they took him off to Holt County to stand trial, ending the honeymoon before it started.

Events in Valentine climbed to such a pitch that Ainsworth, the county seat of Brown County, to the east of Cherry County, called for the transfer of the land office from Valentine to Ainsworth. The Ainsworth paper reported it "is absolutely unsafe for a man to visit Valentine, that he is liable to be knocked down or shot."

Predictably, the *Valentine Reporter* fired back a hot retort, but in the last issue of the paper in 1883, it printed a warning that "the promiscuous shooting upon our streets must be stopped if we want a prosperous town."

After Doc Middleton was arrested and sent to the penitentiary in 1879, Kid Wade

Courtesy Nebraska State Historical Society
The 25th Infantry U.S. Negro Regiment on the parade ground in Fort Niobrara, circa 1905

headed the horse thieves in north central Nebraska. Cherry County did not escape his notice. Albert "Kid" Wade was described as of slender build, of medium height, and having a shambling gait, low forehead and massive jaw.

Kid Wade got in trouble with the law in 1880 for stealing a horse in Iowa. He spent a year in an Iowa prison. When he got out, he came to Nebraska and repeated the offense. In Nebraska, though, he was more cautious, covering his tracks and slipping away each time the law got close.

The vigilantes took up the chase. They were determined men, dedicated to ridding the area of horse thieves. A man who called himself Captain Burnham was leader of the vigilantes. Many people figured that some of the vigilantes were former horse thieves themselves. Henry Richardson was a prominent vigilante—some newspapers claimed he had been a partner of Doc Middleton in the "horse trading" business.

In January of 1884, the vigilantes got word from Carn's Bridge in Brown County, just east of Cherry County, that two horses answering the description of stolen animals had been located there. The vigilantes rushed over.

The men who had notified the vigilantes had taken possession of the animals but the men who had bought them from Kid Wade had reclaimed them. The vigilantes went after those men as though they were accomplices of Wade. They caught up with Henry Brockman first and frightened him into turning over the horse and an additional thirty-five dollars to help pay the vigilantes' expenses.

Then they went after Frank Ellison who also gave them no trouble. Still they were no closer to Kid Wade than before.

Eventually they were informed that Jim Smith knew where the Kid was hiding so they went in search of him. Smith wasn't easy to find but they finally caught up with him. He denied knowing anything about Kid Wade. The vigilantes found a convenient tree and put a noose around Smith's neck.

Smith defiantly denied any knowledge of Wade until he realized they really intended to hang him. Then he broke down and told

Courtesy Nebraska State Historical Society Solomon D. Butcher Collection

"Shorty," an old time cowboy in Cherry County, near Pulman.

them they could find Kid Wade in Le Mars, Iowa.

The vigilantes sent men to Le Mars and, with the help of the sheriff there, they found Wade and brought him back to Nebraska. The vigilantes bombarded him with questions, trying to get information about the other men in his gang.

Wade was reluctant to divulge too much but he did identify some men among the vigilantes he had known while he was stealing horses. That brought quick reaction from those men, of course, and, in the view of Editor Burley Hill of the *Valentine Reporter,* it led to his lynching before he could say too much about certain members of the vigilantes.

Wade was taken to Long Pine in Brown County and put on exhibit there. Long Pine had given the vigilantes money for running down the horse thieves and they felt the people had a right to see the results of their work.

The vigilantes said they would take Wade to Holt County to stand trial but first, they wanted to get all the information from him they could. Some reports suggest they were getting more information about certain people than they wanted.

Reports differ on how Kid Wade got to Bassett. Some say the sheriff from O'Neill came to Long Pine and took him from the vigilantes; others say the vigilantes themselves moved him to Bassett. However, when they got to Bassett, they were too late to catch that day's train to the east—they had to wait for the next day's train. The vigilantes were still trying to glean more information from Wade about members of his gang. The *Reporter* suggested that Wade began recalling a few names and horse stealing escapades involving members of the vigilantes— naturally, those men hushed him up.

Wade was housed in Martin's Hotel, according to one report. Another said he was placed under guard in an old store building. Regardless of where he spent the first half

of the night, there is no argument about where he spent the second half.

About midnight, masked men stormed in, overpowered the guards, and took Wade out into the night. Wade begged them to hear more about his gang but they wouldn't wait to listen. If true, this would verify the charge that Wade was hanged by those vigilantes who didn't want him to divulge his past involvements with them.

He was dragged out and hanged at the whistle signal post along the railroad east of Bassett on February 8, 1884. His father had been killed, apparently by vigilantes, just a few months before. The charge against him had been horse stealing, too.

In 1884, Valentine was the last town on the railroad tracks. This location fostered a tough element in the town that threatened to dominate everything. There was another

Courtesy Nebraska State Historical Society

James C. Dahlman, 1884

element there, though, hankering for the finer things in life. James C. Dahlman was well known in Valentine as the manager of the Newman Cattle Company to the west of town. He and the sheriff of Cherry County, W. H. (Billy) Carter, decided to organize a social club; it would exclude roughnecks from membership. Cherry County at that time encompassed all the northern tier of Nebraska from the Brown County line to the state line touching Wyoming Territory.

The social club was very exclusive. Their first entertainment was by invitation only; this eliminated the wild element. As soon as those individuals heard of the plans, they sent a warning to the social club to invite them or there would be blood on the moon.

Dahlman and Carter did not change their plans. The event began as scheduled—by invitation only. None of the tough guys were present as the party got under way.

Shortly after things began, the front door was knocked off its hinges and a dozen of the roughest men in the country burst inside. They had guns and began shooting at the lights. Within moments, the big room was plunged into darkness. Men and women ran screaming for the windows—most went through, taking sashes with them. Only Dahlman and Carter stayed.

When the shooting stopped, Dahlman found a chair, got up on it and lit a lamp that was still intact. With his gun in hand, he informed the party crashers that he would give them just five minutes to get out of the hall. Anyone who remained after that would never leave it alive. Carter stood to one side holding his gun and backed up Dahlman's threat.

For a minute, it was a stand-off. Then the tough men decided it wasn't worth the price of admission. They dropped their almost-empty guns back into their holsters and faded into the night. Dahlman and Carter brought the invited guests back into the hall and the party proceeded, although most likely on a subdued note.

In January of 1885, Minnechaduza Cemetery got another resident. It was not the man the killer had intended to send there. The killing took place west of Valentine at a grade camp where Cody now stands. A homesteader known as Old Man Murphy and his nephew were going for a load of wood over in the canyons near Boiling Springs on Johnson's ranch. Murphy's nephew was a belligerent young man—he knew that Johnson's cowboys weren't likely to take kindly to homesteaders gathering wood on the ranch. The nephew sharply remarked as they were passing the grade camp that no cowboy was going to stop him from getting the wood he needed.

A cowboy from the ranch, Prosper Merriam, better known as "Frenchy," was at the camp. He took instant exception to the comment and pulled his gun. His obvious intention was to shoot the young man. But Murphy stepped in front of his nephew and he was the man who was killed.

Frenchy was taken to Valentine and put in jail but his friends got him out and sent him where the law couldn't find him. Old Man Murphy was buried in the Minnechaduza Cemetery.

In the cold weather of that winter, another tragedy took place along the Niobrara. There was bad blood between two settlers a little east of Valentine. W. T. Comstock lived on the north side of the river while a man named Smith live just across the ford on the south side.

Smith was a big man—he openly threatened to kill Comstock the first time he came across the river. Comstock didn't hear about the threat and went hunting on the south side. But Smith's neighbor knew and he told Comstock. Comstock decided he'd go back home rather than hunt. However, to get to the ford where everyone crossed the river, Comstock had to go right by Smith's house.

Smith apparently hadn't noticed Comstock when he came across to hunt. He noticed him all too well when he started back home.

He came out, swearing at Comstock and yelling that he would kill him before he got home. Comstock ignored him and trotted his horse out onto the ice across the ford.

Smith ran back into his house and returned with a shotgun. By that time, Comstock was across the river, almost out of range of the shotgun. When Comstock reached the north bank of the river, he swung out of the saddle, threw off his overcoat, and took aim with his rifle. He fired twice and Smith went down.

Smith was hit by both bullets, once in the hip and once in the small of the back. Comstock trotted his horse on home. Smith was carried into his house where he died late that night.

Comstock was arrested. His trial came up in the next court term. He was sentenced to one year in the penitentiary but got out in nine months for good behavior.

Johnny Key had a younger brother called Lank. He was as quick on the trigger as Johnny. One night in the spring of 1885, Lank got into a quarrel with a girl called "Paint" at the Hog Ranche. In their drunken fight, Lank Key pulled his gun and shot her. He skipped the country before the sheriff caught wind of anything and he was never heard from again in Cherry County. But "Paint" became the next resident of the Minnechaduza Cemetery.

The next one to go to the cemetery was sent there by mistake, as Old Man Murphy had been. In May of 1885, Ed McDade, a cousin of the Key brothers, quarreled with Carlie Sickler in a saloon in Valentine. Sickler was a friend of a gambler at the saloon known only as Keno. The quarrel exploded and Sickler drew his gun and shot at McDade. He missed and hit the gambler, Keno, instead. So Keno was taken to the Minnechaduza Cemetery. So far, all the graves in the cemetery were filled with victims of violence.

Several units of the 9th Cavalry were transferred to Fort Niobrara shortly after

Courtesy Nebraska State Historical Society

Gathering cow chips in an old tub or basket, 1896.

Keno's death. The 9th was a Negro unit—
soon there was a settlement of black camp
followers in Valentine, on the south side of
the railroad tracks. Both the town and the
fort bragged that there were no racial problems stemming from the presence of Negro
troops.

That changed in 1887 when a young black
man named Jerry White was arrested for rap-
ing a white woman in Valentine. He was
taken to Long Pine and held in jail. The
hope was that with White in jail at Long
Pine, Valentine's population would not let its
feelings boil over. Long Pine was fifty miles
from Valentine.

No one knew whether the mob came from
Valentine or whether it formed in Long Pine.
But the mob surged in, overpowered the officers, dragged White from the jail and
hanged him.

Some incidents about Valentine were laced
with humor. Arkansas Bob and his friend,
Bill, were drinking in an upstairs saloon and
stayed too long. Bob finally quit and started
to sleep off his drunk but the saloon keeper
told Bill he would have to get him out—his
snores were disturbing the other patrons.
With the help of the saloon keeper, Bill got
Bob out, the saloon keeper slamming the
door behind them.

They were on the platform leading to the
stairs and the street. Arkansas Bob and Bill
stood there, weaving in the wind, waiting for
the stairs to come around so they could make
their way down. Finally, they set themselves
to catch the stairway the next time around;
then together they made for it. They tumbled head over heels to the bottom and
bounced into the middle of the street. When
they recovered, they decided to leave before those stairs attacked them again.

Arm in arm they wandered down the
street, looking for a place where they could
escape the chilly wind. Valentine was not a
big town then and the two soon found themselves out on the prairie. Hand in hand, they

Courtesy Nebraska State Historical Society
The Valentine Alliance

staggered along until suddenly, Bill realized
he was standing alone.

After a minute of looking around dazedly,
Bill called, "Where are ye, Bob?"

"Down here in this well," Bob yelled back.
This second fall had sobered Arkansas Bob
enough to comprehend his situation.

On hands and knees, Bill crawled over to
the edge of the hole and peered down. "How
fur down are ye?" he yelled.

"Forty feet," Bob yelled back. Actually, it
was only fifteen feet. "Find somebody to get
me out."

Bill was still in a happy mood. He started
off for help, but then turned and came back.
Bob was shocked into total sobriety when he
saw Bill sitting on the curbing of the well
and letting his feet dangle over the edge. He

realized only too well what would happen if Bill fell on top of him.

"I told you to go get help," Bob roared.

"I'm going," Bill mumbled. "I just wanted you to promise you'll be here when I get back."

"Of course I'll be here," Bob said, trying not to aggravate the still drunk Bill. Just a strong lean forward and Bill would come crashing down on him.

"All right," Bill said. "But you stay right there till I get back."

Bill got back on solid ground and staggered off toward town. He stumbled into another drinking buddy named Charlie who had a bottle. The two headed back out to the prairie to finish the bottle. Daylight found them south of town and as they wandered back into the outskirts, Bill suddenly remembered his friend Bob in the well. He reported it but he had no idea where the well was.

A search was started and one of the searchers remembered the dry well out by the cemetery. There they found a thoroughly sober Arkansas Bob. He was still there just as he'd promised Bill he would be.

Not all tragedy was the result of guns. A family named Haumann settled in the sandhills south of Valentine. There were several children in the family so the oldest daughter, Hannah, went to work for a neighbor named Gilson a mile and half away. She usually came home on Sundays but on May 10, 1891, she was asked to stay on the job.

Two of her sisters, Tillie, eight years old, and Retta, four, disappointed that Hannah hadn't come home, asked permission to walk over and see her. It was a beautiful spring day so their mother let them go. They were instructed to start back at four o'clock and come straight home.

They skipped away to the neighbors, visited with their sister, and started home at four. Spring flowers were everywhere in the sand hills and they were an irresistable attraction to the little girls. They left the path and picked some flowers.

But there were flowers even prettier a little farther along and they went after them. Soon they were out of sight of the path toward home.

Anyone familiar with the Nebraska sand hills knows that every hill looks identical to every other and they stretch on like waves on a stormy sea. The girls were completely lost, not even sure of the direction toward home.

When the girls were not home by dark, the Haumanns prepared for a search to start at dawn Monday morning. Neighbors were alerted and the men left their fields to join in.

The trail was located just before dark on Monday evening. Some men camped on the trail so they could get an early start. Tuesday was a difficult day for the searchers. Sometimes the trail would be clear where patches of sand revealed the girls' tracks. Other times, the sand was carpeted with grass that hid the tracks.

Tuesday night marked the end of another fruitless search. Only on Wednesday morning did they discover they had camped just a short distance from where the girls had bedded down in the sand for the night. But the girls were up and gone by the time the men arrived.

Sometime Wednesday morning, Tillie, the older girl, told her sister she was going to the top of a big hill ahead and look for a house. Both girls were extremely tired and hungry. Retta was to wait there for Tillie to come back.

But Tillie went on from that big hill toward another one that looked higher just ahead. Retta decided she could save time by going around the hill and meeting Tillie there.

The searchers found Retta about noon, sunburned, famished and almost out of her mind. She could only point vaguely in the direction she thought Tillie had gone.

The search went on for Tillie until Sunday, the 17th, exactly one week from the time the girls had gotten lost. They found

Tillie that day. She had taken off her apron and spread it over a wild rose bush and laid down under it for shade. And there she had died.

The inscription on her tombstone hardly hints of her ordeal. It says simply: "Mathilda L. Haumann born April 14, 1883, died May 17, 1891."

The turn of the century brought little peace to the soldiers of Fort Niobrara. They had no wars to fight but they found plenty of problems in and around the fort, mostly of their own creation.

In March, 1905, Privates Millaman and London of Co. K, 1st Cavalry, went on a rampage in Valentine. At two o'clock in the morning they went to the home of C. H. Thompson, a saloonkeeper, and smashed in the door. It was never determined whether they wanted Thompson to open the saloon again or if they planned to rob the man. They had obviously had too much to drink already. They were about as gentle and quiet in breaking into Thompson's house as a bull turned loose in a tin shop.

Thompson heard their first efforts to break down the door. He jumped out of bed and grabbed his double action .38 revolver. As he dashed into the next room, the front door burst open, knocked off its hinges. Thompson didn't wait for his visitors to identify themselves or explain their mission. He began shooting, firing all five shots in the revolver.

When the smoke cleared, one man was on the floor; the other was staggering away in the direction of the livery stable. Thompson went directly to the city marshal and turned himself in.

Examination showed that both men had been shot in the head. London had been hit three times and was near death. Millaman had been hit twice. His wounds were not so serious and he recovered. Most people in Valentine felt that Thompson was justified in what he did. A few felt that he had acted too hastily.

Thompson's trial came up in court in June of that year. He was found guilty of manslaughter but much sentiment was on his side.

Perhaps the unintentional shooting of the musician, Rothchild, at the Hog Ranche, just outside Valentine, emphasizes best the reckless mode of living in that era. Soney Ford had been a soldier at Fort Niobrara. After his discharge, he got a job driving the stage coach between Valentine and the fort, a short drive but usually carrying several passengers.

On Christmas Eve, 1902, Ford brought a load of passengers to the Hog Ranche on the road between Valentine and Fort Niobrara. He stopped there with his passengers and took part in the holiday festivities. Near the end of the evening, Ford rushed up to the platform where the musician sat playing the piano, shouting that somebody had stolen his overcoat. Ford had a revolver in his hand.

Apparently he had been ready to take his passengers home when he discovered his overcoat missing. He leaped up on the platform, waving his pistol wildly. The musician, Rothchild, tried to calm him.

"Be careful with that pistol," he suggested. "You have your finger on the trigger."

Ford continued to wave the pistol. "I know that. I want to show you how it works."

He squeezed the trigger right in Rothchild's face, killing him almost instantly.

Ford threw down the pistol, pushed back the piano stool, and tried to lift Rothchild to his feet, pleading with the crowd not to hurt him; he hadn't meant to shoot the piano player.

Ford was arrested and accused of murder. At his trial, the jury found him not guilty of first- or second-degree murder, since there had been no premeditation on the stage driver's part. But he was found guilty of manslaughter. His sentence was seven years in the penitentiary which was later reduced to four years.

West of Valentine, a young rancher named Charles Sellers had been courting a neighbor girl, Eunice Murphy, for some time. A quarrel apparently came up between them, but not even the trial in Valentine revealed the cause of the argument.

Eunice lived with her aunt, Mrs. Heath. Also living with Mrs. Heath were Harry Heath and Eunice's brother, Kenneth Murphy. These young men, along with two neighbors, George and Alma Weed, decided to do something about Charles Sellers.

One night in June they went to the house of Jack Hutch, another neighbor, because they knew that Charles Sellers was staying there that night. Hutch and Sellers had already gone to bed but George Weed knocked loud enough to wake Hutch. Since Weed was a friend of Hutch, he was invited in.

Weed said he wanted to talk to Sellers but Sellers said he wasn't feeling well so he didn't get up. In a few minutes, Alma Weed, Kenneth Murphy and Harry Heath came in. The four men demanded that Sellers get up, which he did. Then they put a rope around his neck and started to lead him out of the house. According to Hutch, both he and Sellers thought it was a practical joke or, at most, an attempt to scare Sellers.

The four young men led Sellers out to a telephone pole and hanged him. They came back and told Hutch what they had done. After they left, Hutch hurried out to find that Sellers had indeed been hanged. He sat there through the night to make sure the coyotes didn't get to the body. The sheriff came out from Valentine the next morning and cut down the body.

The four men were arrested and charged with murder. They were hustled to Valentine before any of their friends could interfere and free them. They all came from prominent families in the community and feelings ran high on both sides of the issue. The atmosphere was so charged that Eunice Murphy left to visit relatives in Missouri.

Later, charges of being an accomplice were filed against Eunice Murphy but the authorities couldn't find her in Missouri. She finally returned of her own accord in time for the trial.

The only defense the four men put up was that Charles Sellers had threatened to kill both Kenneth and Eunice Murphy and they had acted in self-defense.

Eunice was released but the four men were sentenced to life imprisonment. They might have been executed but the court allowed them to plead guilty to second-degree murder—over the objections of the prosecuting attorney.

Most confessed murderers admit being sorry that they committed the crime. But the Valentine jail housed one man who was sorry only because he hadn't killed three people instead of just one.

His name was Frank Allen. He hired out to the rancher, William Heckel. He worked only sixteen days and then quit because he said he had been given poisoned food by Heckel and 'Doc' Williams. He went to Casper, Wyoming, where he bought a gun and returned with the firm intention of killing Heckel, and Williams and his wife.

He lay in wait close to Heckel's ranch house for over twenty-four hours. When Heckel finally appeared, Allen stepped out and fired at him four times. Three of the shots hit the rancher, killing him.

When a young woman rushed out of the house, Allen ran inside and tore out the telephone. He took a rifle and some ammunition and then retreated to a nearby marsh to hide.

The entire county was up in arms at the news of the murder of the young rancher. A hundred men banded together and went in search of the killer. Sheriff Colman and County Attorney Heelan stayed with the men, trying to cool their fury.

They located Allen in the marsh and captured him. The posse quickly began transforming itself into a lynch mob, but the sheriff and the county attorney took charge and whisked the prisoner away to the Valentine jail.

Even the threat of the mob failed to dampen the defiance in the prisoner. He maintained he only regretted not having killed Williams and his wife, too. The record of his trial seems to have vanished but it is doubtful that imprisonment changed his attitude.

At a time when it seemed that the days of outlaws and wild crime were past, one of the ugliest murders ever to hit Valentine occurred. It was October, 1915, and shades of the 1880s returned.

The actual site of the double-murder was a few miles southeast of Valentine at a ranch near Arabia. A young man, William Cryderman, about eighteen, was working for John Heelan on his ranch.

Heelan had gone to Omaha to attend the Aksarben festivities. Apparently Mrs. Nellie Heelan had invited Anna Layport to stay with her until her husband returned. Mrs. Layport lived in Valentine.

Cryderman had gone to Arabia for something that afternoon of October 13. Mrs. Heelan and Mrs. Layport were also in Arabia. Cryderman returned to the ranch ahead of the women. When Mrs. Heelan arrived home, she scolded Cryderman for driving a sick horse to town that afternoon.

Some reports say that Cryderman was not overly intelligent, but he went about his business of getting revenge for the scolding with careful planning. He wrote a note and pinned it to a bridle in the barn. It read, "I won't tell what the trouble started over but you will find our bones in the ashes."

Then he got his gun and went to the house. He deliberately shot Mrs. Heelan in the head, apparently killing her instantly. Mrs. Layport ran into the other room to the telephone. She frantically rang it to summon help.

Cryderman ran after her and shot her before she could get an answer to her ring. Then he went outside to the kerosene barrel and got a can of kerosene. Back inside, he poured the kerosene over the bodies of Mrs. Heelan and Mrs. Layport. Some reports said that, according to the way they found the remains among the broken pieces of the telephone, Mrs. Layport was not dead when Cryderman poured the kerosene over her and lit it with a match.

The fire totally destroyed the house. Cryderman lost his nerve and didn't kill himself as he had intended when he wrote the note. He took the fastest horse on the ranch and rode southeast to Wood Lake where he caught a freight train going west. Apparently he figured the law would expect him to flee east.

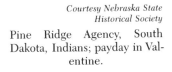

Courtesy Nebraska State Historical Society

Pine Ridge Agency, South Dakota, Indians; payday in Valentine.

John Heelan found the burned house and the bodies the next morning when he returned home. From a neighbor's, he telephoned the authorities in Valentine. They came immediately. When they found Cryderman's note in the barn, they knew who was responsible.

The sheriff rushed back to Valentine, intent on sending telegrams to all stations east and west to watch for the murderer. But when he got there, he found Cryderman himself trying to board a freight train headed west. The train he had boarded at Wood Lake had put him off at Valentine and he was forced to try to hitch another ride on the next train.

News of the murders had spread over the town. Both victims were well known and respected. The fuse was lit. The sheriff realized that the days of lynching could come back in a hurry. He moved fast to get Cryderman in jail and post a heavy guard, not just to keep Cryderman in jail but to keep the incensed citizens out.

Such a crime was worse than anything in Valentine's history. Deliberately murdering two highly respected women and then burning the bodies, apparently before Mrs. Lay-port was dead, was almost more than the citizens could tolerate. Yet they lived now by law and order and the threatened mob did not materialize.

Cryderman's trial came up on March 5, 1916, in Valentine. Sheriff Rosseter still worried about mob violence. Feelings continued to run very high whenever the crime was mentioned. He stationed twenty-five armed men around the courtroom to snuff out any uprising that might erupt. None did.

Cryderman had been examined and pronounced sane so the jury had to make a decision as to his guilt. The jury was out only a few minutes after the case was handed to them following a day and a half trial. The verdict was murder in the first degree.

Judge Westover sentenced Cryderman to death in the electric chair, a penalty that had not come from Cherry County before. The sentence was to be carried out at the state penitentiary on June 23, 1916, between eleven A.M. and three P.M.

Cryderman's trial was swift and short; the sentence was to be carried out only three months later. It was an example for other potential murderers to decide whether revenge was worth it. For Cryderman it wasn't.

Chapter 10

Broken Bow

In its earliest days, Broken Bow, Custer's county seat, was said to be the capital of Nebraska cattle country. It was great ranching country and ranchers were not slow to see that. But it was also good farming country and homesteaders saw that as well. Mixing the interests of these two groups was akin to combining nitric acid and glycerin.

Big cattle outfits moved in on the North, Middle, and South Loup Rivers and their tributaries. One of the biggest was I. P. "Print" Olive's herds from Texas. The Olives came from south and a little east of Dallas. They wanted more room for their growing herds and one of the Olive brothers, Bob, had urgent necessity to flee Texas before the law caught up with him. In Nebraska, he assumed the name Bob Stevens and claimed to be the foreman for Print Olive, his brother.

Starting on Dismal River, they soon moved southeast, eventually establishing headquarters on the South Loup, about four miles east of present-day Callaway and ten or twelve miles southwest of Broken Bow. It wasn't a pretentious headquarters because the Olive brothers, Print, Ira, and Bob, each built a fine house down in Plum Creek in Dawson County where their families lived—they spent most of their time on the ranch in Custer County.

Trouble erupted when homesteaders began crowding in. The area looked good for farming to land-hungry settlers. Times were hard and a few were not above helping themselves to a ranch calf now and then. After all, the ranchers had hundreds of cattle; they could afford the loss of an occasional calf.

The ranchers, however, took a distinctly different view. They hadn't accumulated those herds by letting calves be stolen. Print Olive was the biggest rancher on the South Loup and he squealed the loudest.

One settler, Manley Capel, was caught stealing a ranch calf. At his trial, he implicated another settler, Ami Ketchum. Ketchum was a young single man who made his home with a man in his sixties, Luther Mitchell, and his wife. Suspicion pointed directly at them.

Print Olive was determined to run Ketchum and Mitchell out of the country or have them arrested. Bob Olive (Stevens) was deputized by the sheriff of Buffalo County, Dave Anderson, to arrest Ketchum and Mitchell. This evolved, it seems, when some Olive cattle were sold in Kearney and Bob Olive saw them. He knew that no Olive cattle were for sale so he called the sheriff. They went to the buyer and examined the bill of sale—it had the forged name of Print Olive on it. It also named the men who had delivered the cattle. Ketchum and Mitchell were among them so the sheriff deputized this man "Bob Stevens" to arrest them.

Bob Olive was wearing his deputy sheriff star when he went to Mitchell's place to arrest the pair. Expecting trouble, he took two men with him, Pete Beaton and Barney Armstrong. On the way, he picked up Jim McIndeffer to guide them to the Mitchell homestead, which he had never visited.

Close to the homestead, they stopped and peeked over the last ridge. Ketchum and Mitchell were tying a neighbor's bull to the back of the wagon to take him home. Bob Olive sent Pete Beaton down to separate the men. They had never seen Beaton; they did know Bob Olive. Since Ketchum was a blacksmith, Beaton rode into the yard and asked Ketchum to shoe his horse. Ketchum refused, saying he had to return the bull to Mr. Dowse.

Realizing they couldn't separate the two men, Olive decided on a frontal attack. McIndeffer stayed behind while the other three rode boldly down the slope into the yard. Ketchum and Mitchell barely looked up when Bob Olive shouted that as a deputy sheriff he was arresting them. He called for them to throw up their hands. Instead,

Ketchum jerked up his six-gun. He and Olive exchanged shots. Beaton and Armstrong joined the shooting; Ketchum's left arm was broken but he kept fighting.

Mitchell grabbed his rifle and took dead aim at Bob Olive. Olive saw him and yelled just before he pulled the trigger but yelling didn't stop the bullet. Only the quick move of his two companions kept Olive from falling out of the saddle.

By now Ketchum's six-gun was out of ammunition. Beaton and Armstrong wheeled their horses and, holding Bob Olive in the saddle, galloped back over the hill. Ketchum grabbed Mitchell's rifle and pumped shots after the retreating trio. His aim was bad, likely thrown off by his inability to use his left arm.

Ketchum and Mitchell, realizing the trouble they were in, cut the bull loose, loaded a few belongings from the soddy, and headed

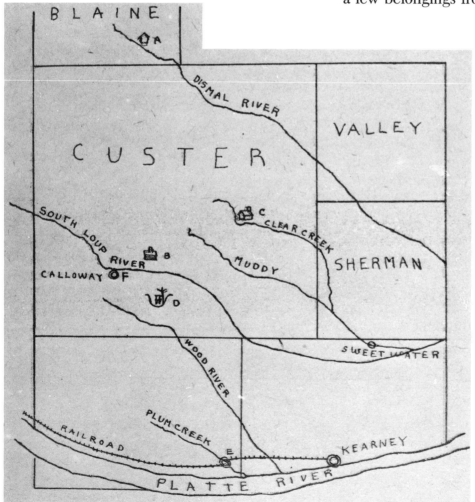

Courtesy Nebraska State Historical Society

Map of the area where the Olive gang hung out. (B) Print Olive's ranch. (E) Plum Creek (Lexington) where the Olive family lived. (C) Mitchell Homestead.

east toward Merrick County where they had previously lived.

Beaton and Armstrong took Olive to the home of a settler named Frank Harrington down Clear Creek from Mitchell's homestead. There he made out his will and three days later he died.

As soon as word got to Print Olive's ranch that Bob Olive had been shot, a posse of cowboys rode to Mitchell's soddy but no one was there. They burned the roof of the soddy—the only flammable part.

Print Olive offered a reward of seven hundred dollars for the delivery of Mitchell and Ketchum. He obtained a warrant for their arrest and gave it to Barney Gillan, sheriff of Keith County, who had come from Ogallala to get in on the manhunt. Three other sheriffs were involved in the search, including Sheriff Dave Anderson of Buffalo County, who had deputized Bob Olive. Sheriffs E. W. Crew of Howard County and William Letcher of Merrick County eventually found Mitchell and Ketchum and arrested them.

The two sheriffs took the prisoners to Kearney where there was a good jail. Then began the jockeying to claim the reward from Print Olive. However, Print made it clear that the reward was not due until the prisoners were delivered to him in Custer County.

Sheriffs Crew and Letcher refused to turn the prisoners over to Print Olive, knowing they would almost certainly be lynched. Sheriff Anderson also refused. But Barney Gillan, sheriff of Keith County, arrived and agreed to take them. He had the warrant Print had sworn out and his eye was on that seven hundred-dollar reward. He took Phil DuFran, deputy sheriff of Custer County, with him to guard the prisoners.

Lawyers tried to stop the prisoners' transfer to Custer County but when the train pulled into Lexington, Print Olive was at the depot with a couple of wagons. Mitchell and Ketchum were loaded into a wagon and whisked out of town, heading north toward the Custer County line. A few men from Lexington rode along, eager for some excitement.

Sometime before noon the next day, the wagon carrying the prisoners reached a dividing point in the trail: one road went to Print Olive's ranch and the other to a neighboring ranch. Here Print and several of his men, including two who had ridden out from Lexington, conferred with Sheriff Gillan and Deputy DuFran and the two officers turned the prisoners over to Olive's men. They ap-

Courtesy Nebraska State Historical Society Solomon D. Butcher Collection

Old Mitchell sod house where Ketchum killed Olive in 1878. Clear Creek used to run near the old Mitchell place.

Courtesy Nebraska State Historical Society
Solomon D. Butcher Collection

Mitchell and Ketchum homestead, east Custer County, 1888 or 1889

parently were given the seven hundred dollars reward money and split it between them.

Print led the way up a canyon toward a spot called Devil's Gap. This is about five miles southeast of present-day Callaway and only a short distance from Print's ranch. They stopped the wagon beneath an elm tree. Ropes were thrown over a limb and nooses fit over the heads of the prisoners. Print Olive shot Mitchell in the side with a rifle just as Mitchell had shot Bob Olive. Then both men were hanged. The men went on to the ranch.

No one is sure who burned the bodies of the hanged men but it is assumed that the two men from Lexington were guilty. They were plenty drunk when they left Olive's ranch. With their gallon jug still partly full of whisky, they left in high spirits.

Their way back to town went right down

*Courtesy Nebraska State
Historical Society
Solomon D. Butcher Collection*
Hartington, the first house south of old Mitchell ranch where the cowboys took Bob Olive after he was shot. Olive died here three days later.

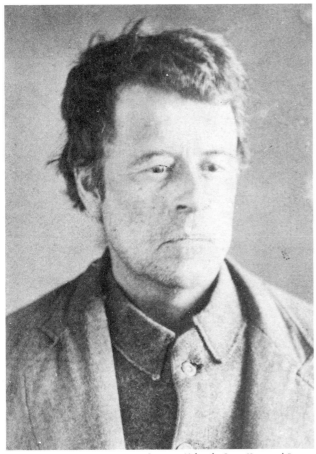

I. P. "Print" Olive, penitentiary photo

Olive family grave markers

the canyon where Mitchell and Ketchum had been hanged. When the bodies were found the next afternoon, they were burned black. The fire had spread to the grass but had been beaten out to prevent it from starting a prai-

rie fire. Speculation was that the two men poured their remaining whisky over the bodies and set them on fire. Then they sobered up enough to realize they had to stop the fire from spreading and had beaten it out.

That was not the story that circulated through the country then, however. The blame for the hangings and the burning was laid on Print Olive. He was dubbed the man burner. Print was convicted and sent to the Nebraska penitentiary for lynching and burning the two men.

After his release, Print Olive returned to Kansas. On August 16, 1886, he was shot to

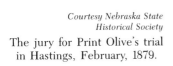

The jury for Print Olive's trial in Hastings, February, 1879.

death in Trail City, Colorado, on the Kansas-Colorado border, by a worthless gunman named Joe Sparrow. Olive, unarmed when he was gunned down, was forty-six years old.

A potentially explosive situation arose between the Brighton ranch some distance outside Broken Bow and the settlers who came in and claimed the free government land. Even though it was 1884 and the settlers had been coming slowly into Custer County for some time, the Brighton ranch fences ran around its grazing land, mainly to discourage homesteaders.

But not all settlers were frightened off by the fences. They simply went through them, chose their land, and began plowing sod for their houses. Broken Bow was well on its way to becoming sod house capital of the world. Reporters who came into the county claimed there were more sod houses in Custer County than anywhere else on earth. They were never disputed.

The settlers on the Brighton ranch sent notice to the ranch headquarters to come and take down their fences. Of course, they ignored the request. The settlers considered this refusal solid grounds for removing the fences themselves. Since they were still building their soddies and the posts looked like good rafters for their houses, they proceeded to use them as such, laying the posts from the side walls to the ridge poles and piling brush over them. Two layers of sod went over the brush, followed with yellow clay found not far away. That clay would turn water almost as well as shingles.

When the ranch owners discovered their fences torn down and the posts used to build sod houses, they proceeded to Broken Bow and got the sheriff. He came out and arrested every settler who had used the posts in his house.

The foreman of the Brighton ranch went to town to swear out complaints against the settlers. In the meantime, he had left word for his second in command to retrieve the posts. Taking a group of cowboys just in case of trouble, the substitute foreman went about his task with relish.

Courtesy Nebraska State
Historical Society
Solomon D. Butcher Collection

The Davis homestead on Clear Creek near the Mitchell ranch, 1887.

He hitched up a big wagon, took plenty of ropes and headed for the homesteads. Throwing a rope over the end of the ridge pole of a soddy, he whipped the term into a run, tearing out the ridge pole and scattering posts in every direction. The dirt roof caved in on the household goods below. The cowboys gathered up the posts and then dashed on to the next soddy to repeat the destruction.

One homestead mother sent her boy to town on the saddle horse to tell the sheriff what was transpiring. In the meantime, the cowboys proceeded along the neighborhood, wrecking each soddy to get their posts.

The foreman in Broken Bow heard the homestead boy's report and dispatched one of his men to tell the cowboys to get away from the soddies fast. The messenger found the cowboys and warned them that a posse of angry men was forming in town and would be coming soon. The cowboys abandoned the soddies and whipped their horses toward the hills to prepare for a battle with the posse. They drove so fast that posts bounced out of the wagon at every bump. When the team began to tire, the cowboys threw posts overboard to lighten the load. They wanted to reach the hills before being overtaken.

In town the ranchers failed to make a case against the settlers because the land was gov-ernment land and the fences were illegal. The farmers, on the other hand, didn't press charges for destroying their houses. The fences were removed and the homesteaders settled down to breaking sod and planting crops. After waiting three days in the hills for the anticipated battle, the cowboys came sneaking back to the ranch and the incident was not mentioned again.

The following spring trouble erupted again on what was formerly the Brighton ranch. A man named Joseph Province settled on one of the quarters of land that was once fenced by the ranch. He had barely gotten settled when one of the hands working on the Brighton ranch, Stephen Long, appeared to tell him he had relinquishment rights from the Brighton cowboy who had taken a pre-emption on the quarter. Province didn't believe him and kept his land.

As Province was just finishing his sod house Long proceeded to build a house for himself on the same quarter just a short distance away. Hot words were exchanged between the two whenever they met, which was often.

Long was single but he had a man and his wife living with him, Charles and Maria Powell. Province had several boys, some of them old enough to work in the field.

Courtesy Callaway Centennial Commission

Conflicts between settlers and ranchers.

The case was referred to the land office to determine which man had legal right to the land. The land office delayed its decision. In the meantime, the situation on the homestead was becoming more explosive. Long and Powell began carrying guns when they left their house and Province did the same.

Joseph Province had to go to town one day in early April. He left his two oldest sons, twelve and fourteen, to plow the sod ready for planting a crop. Stephen Long appeared at the field with a Winchester rifle and ordered the boys to stop plowing or he would shoot. They quickly unhitched their teams and one rode to town to tell his father what had happened.

Joseph Province was advised not to bring the law into it since no real crime had been committed. The next morning, he took his oldest son with him when he went out to resume plowing. He also took a revolver and a shotgun.

Shortly after the two got to the field, Long and Powell came out. Long had a repeating rifle and Powell a needle gun. They began shooting at the two in the field and Province fired back with his revolver. Long and Powell took shelter but continued to shoot. Province fired his shotgun and apparently ran out of ammunition for his revolver. He started for the house and had gone only a short distance when he went down, mortally wounded with a rifle bullet in his back.

A neighbor rode hard into Broken Bow to report that Province had been shot. Dr. Hull—also the county coroner—summoned a jury and went out to the homestead where the jury listened to all available evidence and concluded that Province had been shot by either Long or Powell and that the attack was not in self-defense.

That verdict was enough to send Stephen Long and Charles Powell into hiding. They went first to the home of Virgil Allyn, foreman of the Brighton ranch, and from there rode into the hills until the furor died down.

However, it didn't die down. When Sheriff C. O. Foote arrived on the scene the next morning, he discovered about seventy-five neighbors gathered at the Province home. There was lynch talk in the air. The sheriff

Courtesy Nebraska State Historical Society Solomon D. Butcher Collection

Old Brighten ranch, 1892

advised them to go home but they promptly got up a petition and signed it, demanding the sheriff resign on the spot. He ignored it.

Then a messenger rode down from the hills with a note to the sheriff from the killers. They offered to give themselves up if they were guaranteed safety from the mob. The mob grudgingly backed down and the sheriff went out and arrested Long and Powell and took them to jail.

The mob at Province's place didn't break up as ordered but went down the creek to what was called the White House, the headquarters of the Brighton ranch. Virgil Allyn, the foreman, was in Broken Bow. The mob proceeded to break into the supplies and enjoy a feast like homesteaders seldom got. Somebody found a keg of ancient wine, but an old man, seeing the potential trouble coming from drunken men already inflamed over the murder, grabbed a hatchet and broke the keg open, spilling the liquor on the ground.

The men, sobered by that act, started for home. On the way though, they passed a log cabin belonging to the Brighton ranch and set it on fire, burning it to the ground. A messenger had raced to Broken Bow to tell Allyn of the uproar and he gathered a group of his cowboys and rode back home as fast as he could. But the mob was gone and a real battle was avoided.

At the trial, Stephen Long was found guilty, Charles Powell, not guilty. Long was sentenced to the penitentiary. A couple of years later, he was released because of poor health. He died a month later.

The first railroad into Custer County came from the southeast into Broken Bow. Mason City was the first town on the railroad inside Custer County. The conductor made it a point when announcing the train's arrival in Mason City to soothe the passenger's nerves by declaring, "You have now crossed the Custer County line; prepare to meet your God."

Broken Bow seemed to be trying to measure up to that reputation. One man lost his life and another went to prison over quarrels about livestock running in the streets of Broken Bow.

Another shooting without such drastic results again occurred over livestock. A team of horses belonging to John Sanderson strayed and a neighbor with a reputation for making trouble found them and decided to take them in and collect damages. Harry was going to town with a load of hay so he led the team behind the load.

At the edge of town, however, John Sanderson met him, recognized his horses, and tried to take them. Harry was carrying a small .22 caliber revolver—he whipped it out and began shooting at Sanderson. Sanderson dropped over, apparently dead, and Harry was horrified at what he'd done. He whipped his horses into a run and drove directly to the sheriff's office. Throwing himself off the load of hay, he ran inside and blurted out to the sheriff that he had murdered a man and was surrendering.

Before the sheriff could formally arrest him, John Sanderson came in the door. Blood trickled from one arm but he was little the worse for the shooting. He walked up to Harry and vigorously shook a finger in his face.

"See here, young man," he said, "if you ever do that again, I'll slap your face."

When the shooting had started, he had thrown up an arm and been hit there but

Courtesy Nebraska State Historical Society
Building the Burlington Road through Custer County, 1887

then he'd dropped down to wait for the shooting to stop. Harry wasn't arrested but he wasn't likely to be so liberal with his shooting after that.

A four-man posse from Brown County, north of Custer County, tracked a pair of renegades, Bohannan and Arnold, south. They stopped at Sargent, northeast of Broken Bow, to inquire whether they'd been seen in town. Bob McGregor, the man they asked, told them he'd seen two men go through. The posse hurried away and overtook the renegades not far from Sargent.

Bohannan and Arnold evidently were unaware their pursuers were so close, judging from their startled looks as two men from the posse charged up, one on either side, and ordered them to throw up their hands.

Bohannan apparently was unarmed but Arnold had a gun strapped around his waist and a Winchester rifle in his saddle boot. Bohannan threw up his hands but Arnold whipped up his revolver. He and Harris, one of the possemen, fired at the same time. Then Harris fired a second time. That shot knocked Arnold off his horse and the gun slipped from his fingers.

Arnold's horse bolted and came alongside Bohannan who reached over to jerk the rifle out of his partner's boot. Davis, the second posseman, had been firing at the outlaws, apparently with no effect. He was closest to Bohannan and saw the outlaw swinging up the rifle. He knew his number was on that bullet if Bohannan got the rifle up to his shoulder.

Spurring his horse up against Bohannan, he stuck his empty revolver in the man's face and yelled for him to drop the rifle or he'd blow his head off. Bohannan had no idea the gun was empty so he let the rifle drop.

The other two possemen advanced then and they all rode back to Sargent with one prisoner, leaving Arnold where he had fallen. The men in Sargent weren't sure if the Brown County men's story was true so they called the sheriff in Broken Bow. The two

possemen who had not been involved in the shooting were allowed to go on home.

Harris, the man who had shot Arnold, was furious at the delay but Arnold had shot him in the shoulder so he allowed the doctor to take care of that wound.

Sheriff Penn arrived, an autopsy was performed on Arnold, and the decision was that Harris had shot in self-defense. It was learned that both Arnold and Bohannan were wanted in other counties for crimes. There was a hundred-dollar reward for the capture of Bohannan.

In the summer of 1887, a pair of brazen thieves invaded Broken Bow and its surrounding territory—raiding farms and ranches, stealing whatever struck their fancy and driving away. A warrant for the thieves' arrest, names unknown, was sworn out by Limon Landis after they pilfered thirty-six dollars worth of harness from him and a set of carpenter tools from a neighbor, Henry Schuette.

Sheriff Penn was absent from the county at the time so the warrant was passed over to Fred Jephcott, constable of Noel, and L. M. Holman, constable of Callaway. The two constables trailed the thieves by listening along the way to accounts of things stolen.

The trail got easier to follow after the thieves 'replaced' their old wagon with one from a farm. The second was a better wagon but it had a loose tire and a wire had been wrapped around it to secure it to the felloe. The wire made a mark on the ground every time the wheel turned.

Still the constables couldn't quite overtake the thieves. Finally they realized the thieves were doubling back, moving from Anselmo toward Merna and Broken Bow. The constables were bone tired and hungry. They went back to Broken Bow for more men and to get some much needed food and rest.

In late afternoon, with additional deputies, they resumed their search. This time they went in two wagons. At the mouth of a can-

The Globe Hotel at Broken Bow

yon only about six miles north of Broken Bow, they met a man who told them that two men in a loaded wagon were approaching. He was sure they were the thieves. The constables divided forces, one wagon veering to the right, the other to the left.

When the wagon drove up, Constable Jephcott ordered the men to halt. He informed them that he represented the law and was arresting them. They ignored the order and kept going. It was deep dusk by this time but the constables could see rifles hanging on the bows of the wagon which had no covering. A saddle horse was tied to the rear.

After the third warning was ignored, they saw one man reach for a rifle. The constable yelled for his men to open fire. Guns roared. One of the thieves jerked forward and fell off the wagon. The other one dropped to the bed of the wagon and lashed the team into a hard run.

One wagonload of officers went after the runaway team and caught it a mile down the canyon. The saddle horse and thief were gone but they recovered the load of stolen goods. There were guns, saddles, clocks, silk handkerchiefs, carpentry tools and many other items in the loot.

The man who had fallen off the wagon was

dead. He was a Mexican. A coroner jury reviewed the facts and declared the killing justified.

That same year, two cowboys, Hugh Fitzpatrick and Billy Degan, boarded a train at Linscott, on the southern edge of Blaine County, and headed for Anselmo. They were on a spree and proceeded to terrorize the passengers with a show of their gun skills. (Coincidentally, the new postmaster at Broken Bow, L. H. Jewett, was on the same train. It was a rough introduction to the country for him.)

Fitzpatrick and Degan were disappointed when they reached Anselmo to find that the town had heard of their coming and had closed its two saloons. What fun could they have with the saloons closed? It took liquor to put zest into painting a town. One saloon was opened in the afternoon by the owner's brother. From then on, the cowboys had all the 'whistle-grease' they needed to turn the town upside down.

The trains coming through were sent on without replenishing the water in their boilers because one cowboy, Billy Degan, was using the pump house for target practice. He was also setting cans on posts and blazing away at them, regardless of what was behind the posts.

When one of Degan's wild shots hit a man in the toe the citizens decided they had had enough. They sent word to Broken Bow for Sheriff Penn to come and quiet things down.

While the town was waiting for the sheriff, the cowboys got two old horses from the livery stable and decided to put the finishing touches on their spree. They rode into two of the stores and helped themselves to the cigars and any other trinkets that pleased their eyes. Then they rode back to the saloon to finish off the day.

By this time Sheriff Penn had arrived. Word reached the two cowboys and they rode their old horses out of the saloon, firing one last shot as a sort of period to the day. Then they left town.

The sheriff and his men followed. It would be no problem to catch them on the old nags they were riding. They stopped at the hand-car house northwest of town. The sheriff stopped his men at a building some distance away to determine the cowboys' intentions. If they continued on out of town, they would not be obstructed.

But after a time, the two cowboys turned their old horses and began riding slowly toward the sheriff and his deputies. Sheriff Penn gave orders to call for them to halt. If they didn't, shoot the horses, not the men.

When they got close, the order was given to halt. They ignored the order and kept coming. People who had followed the sheriff from town now witnessed the result of the cowboys' bravado. The first shots were fired at the horses.

Fitzpatrick's horse went wild when the first shot hit him. The cowboy apparently reached around to grab the back of the saddle to hold himself on the horse. One of the deputies, thinking he was reaching for a gun, shot him through the heart. The other cowboy was thrown from his horse when it fell. He came up running toward the officers with a gun and met the same fate as his partner.

An inquest held shortly afterward declared that the cowboys had been killed while resisting arrest and the case was closed.

Not all calamities in Broken Bow were caused by guns or short ropes and long drops. F. W. Carlin was driving his team home late one evening in mid-August when one horse suddenly shied away from something. Carlin stopped the horses and got out, walking along the side of the horse to see what was wrong.

It was a dark night. He had almost reached the head of the horse when he stepped into thin air. He shot downward like a falling rock. Instantly, he knew what had happened. He had been aware that he was passing an abandoned homestead but he hadn't realized the team had wandered near the dug well.

As the fall continued and his speed increased, he was certain he would be killed when he hit the bottom. His arms were above his head and he kept them there. To reach out would mean broken arms.

Then he hit bottom, his feet plunging into water and mud and water closing over his head. He was amazed he wasn't dead from the impact but the water and mud had slowed his speed. Struggling to free his feet from the mud, he managed to get his head above water where he could breathe. One ankle was already beginning to throb—he knew it was either broken or badly sprained.

Looking up, he could see a tiny circle of light far above. Dark as the night on the prairie was, it was lighter than the depth of the well. It was a very deep well and he perceived his chances of getting out were practically nil. Now that his feet were free, he stood in water up to his armpits. The curbing in the well was slick with slime—each time he tried to climb out of the water, he fell back.

Finally, he found a piece of the curbing he could break off. Locating cracks in the curbing where he could wedge the ends of the board, he made a seat for himself where he could be up out of the water. Struggling

Broken Bow, Custer County

up on the board, he sat there, waiting out the night.

Sometime in the night, he heard his team run away. He felt sure that sealed his doom.

As long as the horses stood by the well, someone might see them and come to investigate. Now there was nothing to alert anyone to his prison. He was at least a mile and a half from any occupied house and no one knew he had come this way on his road home.

By the time the sky brightened above him, he had decided his ankle was badly sprained but not broken. He also had a pain in his back. Looking up, he thought the well was like a gigantic flue to a small patch of blue sky far above. He guessed it was one hundred and fifty feet to the top of the well.

He examined the curbing. The well was about three feet square. Above him were patches of wall without curbing but most of the wall was curbed. The boards were too slimy for him to climb up without hand and footholds.

He remembered his knife and wondered if it had fallen out of his pocket in his struggles to get out of the water. Reaching into his pocket he found it and immediately began carving finger and toeholds in the slimy curbing. It was slow work but he inched his way up a foot or two at a time. He resolved not to back down unless he fell.

When he reached the top of the first tier of curbing, he positioned a board across one corner and rested. Cutting holds in the softer dirt was faster and he soon reached the next curbing where he had to carve notches in the wood. It wasn't as slimy this far above the water but the wood was drier and harder to carve.

As the afternoon light faded, Carlin estimated he had climbed about fifty feet. But it was a lot farther than that to the top and he had reached some curbing that was solid one-by-six boards—he doubted he could cut hand- and toeholds in them. He carved cracks for a board he tore free and made a seat for himself.

He figured he would have to wait for rescue; he could climb no farther. His injured ankle made climbing almost impossible. Night settled in, dropping a black blanket down the well shaft.

Carlin spent the night on his makeshift seat. When morning came, he began calling for help in the chance that someone might ride by close enough to hear him. By mid-forenoon, he realized there was to be no rescue for him.

Thoughts of his wife and little boy overwhelmed him. They were probably frantic now because the team of horses had surely returned home and no one would know where he was. He envisioned his boy racing to meet him when he came home from the field or town. He would have no father to help him grow up now. His wife would be a widow, unable to do the work on the farm.

He resolved he wouldn't wait to die. He'd get out or be killed in the attempt. Using sand on a board for a grindstone, he sharpened his knife and began work on the tightly fitted boards of the curbing and gradually got to the top of that section of curbing.

From there the climbing went easier, except he had to lift all his weight on one foot. He had hopes of getting out until he reached a spot about fifteen or twenty feet from the top. There the curbing stood out from the wall where rainwater had washed away the dirt behind it.

He had only to glance at that curbing hanging there by pegs at the top to realize that, if he tried to put his weight on it, it would come loose and he would crash all the way to the bottom again. A fleeting thought struck him that this might be an easier way to die than to starve to death within twenty feet of freedom.

Then another idea hit him. If the dirt was soft enough to wash away, maybe he could dig a path behind the curbing and climb up to the top on the dirt itself. It wasn't safe but neither was doing nothing. So he began digging, pulling himself in behind the curbing and tunneling his way upward.

It went fairly quickly and before the day ended, he reached the prairie. He had never expected to see the sun again. But now the sun itself seemed to turn against him. He had been in the well two nights and two days without food or water and had barely missed either. Now that the sun was beating down on him, his thirst became almost unbearable. He couldn't walk on his swollen ankle and he was still a long way from any occupied homestead.

He dragged himself out to the same road his team had wandered away from the other night. He waited through the late afternoon for somebody to come by but no one did.

At dusk, he began dragging himself along the road but the pain in his ankle and back forced him to give up and he passed another miserable night but the ground was much more comfortable than the crude little seats he had used the two nights in the well.

Feeling better at daylight, he began dragging himself again and finally got to the home of homesteader Charles Francis. They took him in and gave him food and water. They tried to ease the pain in his back, which proved to be a broken rib, as well as his ankle.

Carlin learned that the hazardous well was 145 feet. His frightening experienced helped effect a law requiring any homesteader who was abandoning his claim to fill his dug well.

The murders of Hiram Roten and William Ashley in Grant Precinct were two of the most senseless of any ever committed in Custer County.

Albert Haunstine was a respected man in the community. Few realized he had tendencies to appropriate things that didn't belong to him. It came to light when a clock and some lumber were missing from the schoolhouse. Other items had disappeared occasionally but nobody suspected a neighbor.

Roten and Ashley, members of the school board, decided they would find the culprit if possible. Wagon tracks leaving the school house had not been erased by recent travel.

The two men followed the tracks to Haunstine's home. When confronted with the accusation, Haunstine admitted taking the clock from the schoolhouse and turned it over to the board members. There were no angry words exchanged during the confrontation and the two men went back toward their wagon. Haunstine took down his rifle and shot both men in the back, killing them instantly.

Haunstine then stole what money was on the bodies, as well as their watches and guns. A neighboring soddy was vacant so he tied the team of horses inside where they wouldn't be noticed by passersby. Then he

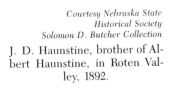

Courtesy Nebraska State Historical Society Solomon D. Butcher Collection

J. D. Haunstine, brother of Albert Haunstine, in Roten Valley, 1892.

got his wife, loaded the few things he wanted to take with him, and drove off to the east. He got a job shucking corn near Madison in northeastern Nebraska.

Shortly after Haunstine left the county, neighbors began to wonder what had happened to Hiram Roten and William Ashley. A search party soon found Haunstine's house vacated. The bodies were located only a short distance away, covered with hay. It didn't take a detective to decide who had killed them. Now came the task of finding Albert Haunstine.

Haunstine was not enthralled with the job of picking corn and sent his wife on to Columbus, telling her he'd be along shortly. A day or two later he boarded the train at Madison to go south to Columbus. Just before it reached its destination, the train was flagged down and boarded by some men. They caught Haunstine in the smoker with a rifle on his lap. The surprise was so effective, he had no chance to use the rifle. He hadn't expected the men from Custer County to follow him here.

Ten years earlier, with the evidence as strong as it was, Haunstine would have been given a short rope and a long drop immediately. But the wheels of justice were grinding out every detail now before any decision was reached. Haunstine was brought back to Custer County and tried in the March term of court. He was found guilty as seemed inevitable and sentenced to be hanged on September 6, 1889.

However, the case was appealed to a higher court by Haunstine's lawyer thereby dragging on for more than a year. Eventually it came up and the decision of the lower court was upheld. The date of the hanging was reset, this time for April 17, 1891.

Haunstine's defense was insanity but the Custer County jury would not declare him insane when he obviously hadn't been at the time of the trial.

However, as the time of execution drew near, Haunstine began acting so strangely that a jury was called to determine his sanity. The trial lasted three days. Indignation festered among the citizens as the possibility grew that Haunstine might be declared insane and escape the gallows. The jury brought in the verdict at two o'clock in the morning. They had found Haunstine sane;

Courtesy Nebraska State Historical Society

Custer County's first courthouse

his strange actions were considered to have been staged.

The verdict came on the morning set for the hanging. A crowd had gathered to witness justice done. Then a rumor filtered through the crowd that Governor Boyd had granted the condemned man a reprieve of thirty days. An angry murmur rose. If a reprieve had been granted, it could mean that Haunstine would escape the gallows yet.

The crowd was rapidly turning into a lynch mob. The people had come to witness the murderer's hanging and they were in no mood to be denied. Only the timely intervention of Judge Hamer who had sat on the bench during the trial held the mob in check. He explained that, in the case of a question of sanity, the law demanded a delay of sentence until the question was removed.

Even that did not set well with the people. So far as they were concerned, the question had been removed. The judge assured them the sentence would be carried out legally and pleaded with them to wait for justice according to law.

The judge himself and two other men traveled to Lincoln to see the governor. Governor Boyd assured them he would place no more obstacles in the way of the wheels of justice. He would not have granted the thirty-day reprieve if he had known the jury had judged the prisoner sane.

Thirty days later, the new day set for the execution rolled around. Broken Bow filled to capacity early in the morning and the crowd began moving close to the courtyard by nine o'clock. It was estimated that two thousand people were there by noon. A high board fence had been built around the yard to hide the gallows. Still the people pressed against the fence even though they couldn't see much.

About 12:30, a man climbed to the top of the fence and threw a block of wood over into the courtyard. This apparently was a signal because, with a whoop, about fifty men rushed forward and slammed into the wooden fence. In less than half a minute, the fence was flat on the ground and the gallows stood naked before the spectators.

The sheriff came out a few minutes later and asked the crowd to stay behind the flattened fence—they agreed now that they could see. The hanging came off as scheduled and those who believed that an eye for an eye was true justice were satisfied. Broken Bow had marked the end of another violent episode in its colorful history.

Bibliography

Adams, Andy. *The Log of a Cowboy. A Narrative of the Old Trail Days*. Boston: Houghton Mifflin, 1903. Lincoln: University of Nebraska Press.

Adamson, Archibald R. *North Platte and its Associations*. North Platte: Evening Telegraph, 1910.

Alberts, Frances Jacobs, ed. *Sod House Memories*. Vols. 1, 2, 3. Hastings: Sod House Society, 1972.

Andreas, Alfred Theodore. *History of the State of Nebraska*. Chicago: Western Historical Company, 1882 (reprint).

Bang, Roy E. *Heroes Without Medals. A Pioneer History of Kearney County, Nebraska*. Minden: Warp Publishing Company, 1952.

Bare, Ira L. and Will H. McDonald. *Illustrated History of Lincoln County, Nebraska, and its People*. Vol. 1. Chicago and New York: American Historical Society, 1920.

Burkley, Frank J. *Faded Frontier*. Omaha: Burkley Envelope and Printing Company, 1935.

Burton, Sir Richard. *The Look of the West, 1860, Across the Plains to California*. London: Longman Green, 1862. Lincoln: University of Nebraska Press.

Carson, John. *Doc Middleton. The Wickedest Outlaw*. Santa Fe: Press of the Territorial, 1966.

Cherry County Extension Council. *Potluck Papers*. Valentine: Cherry County Extension Council, 1974.

Chrisman, Harry E. *The Ladder of Rivers. The Story of I. P. (Print) Olive*. Denver: Sage Books, 1962.

Culbertson Garden Club. *Culbertson Centennial Album*. Culbertson: Culbertson Garden Club, 1973.

Custer, General George A. *My Life on the Plains*. Chicago: Lakeside Press, 1952 (reprint).

Emmett, Chris. *Shanghai Pierce. A Fair Likeness*. Norman: University of Oklahoma Press, 1953.

Fletcher, Don. *How the West was Lost. History of Ogallala*. Aberdeen: North Plains, 1969.

Faulkner, Virginia, ed. *Roundup: A Nebraska Reader*. Lincoln and London: University of Nebraska Press, 1957.

Fitzpatrick, Lilian L. *Nebraska Place Names*. Lincoln: University of Nebraska Press, 1960.

Fuller, Clark. *Pioneer Paths*. Broken Bow: Purcells, 1972.

Gaston, W. L. and Humphrey, A. R. *History of Custer County, Nebraska*. Lincoln: Western Publishing and Engraving Company, 1919.

Grange, Roger T., Jr. *Fort Robinson, Outpost on the Plains*. Lincoln: Nebraska State Historical Society, 1958.

Gressley, Gene, ed. *The American West, A Reorientation*. Laramie: University of Wyoming, 1966.

Grinnell, George, Bird. *The Fighting Cheyennes. The Civilization of the American Indian Series*, No. 44. New York: Charles Scribner's Sons, 1915. Norman: University of Oklahoma Press, 1956.

Herminghausen, F. W. *Tragedy of the Platte Valley*. Kansas City, MO: John Reed Printing Company, 1915.

Hunt, N. Jane, ed. *Nebraska Historical Markers and Sites*. Sioux Falls: Brevet Press, 1974.

Hutton, Harold. *Doc Middleton. Life and Legends of the Notorious Plains Outlaw*. Chicago: Swallow Press, 1974.

Kearney Professional Women. *Where the Buffalo Roamed*. Shenandoah, IA: World Publishing, 1967.

Lass, William E. *From the Missouri to the Great Salt Lake. An Account of Overland Freighting*. Lincoln: Nebraska State Historical Society, 1972.

Mattes, Merrill J. *The Great Platte River Road. The Covered Wagon Mainline via Fort Kearny to Fort Laramie*. Lincoln: Nebraska State Historical Society, 1969.

Metre, Olive Van. *The Old Town, 1880–1889*. North Country Series, Vol. 1. Norfolk, NE: Norfolk Printing, 1977.

Nelson, John Young. *Fifty Years on the Trail*. Norman: University of Oklahoma Press, 1963.

Newton, Mrs. Mary B. *Anecdotes of Omaha*. Omaha: Festner Printing Company, 1891.

Nielson, Elaine. *Ogallala, A Century on the Trail*. Ogallala: Keith County Historical Society, 1984.

O'Gara, E. H. *In All Its Fury. A History of the Blizzard of January 12, 1888*. Lincoln: Dorothy Jenkins, 1947.

Olson, James C. *History of Nebraska*. Lincoln: University of Nebraska Press, 1955.

Parkman, Francis. *The Oregon Trail*. New York: Doubleday, Doran and Company, 1945.

Perkey, Elton A. *Perkey's Nebraska Place Names*. Lincoln: Nebraska State Historical Society, 1982.

Quaife, Milo Milton. *Vanished Arizona, Recollections of My Army Life*. Chicago: Lakeside Press, 1939.

Rhoads, Minnie Alice. *A Stream Called Deadhorse*. Chadron, NE.

Sandoz, Mari. *Old Jules*. New York: Hastings House, 1935. Lincoln: Bison Books, 1962.

———. *The Cattlemen. From the Rio Grande Across the Far Marias*. New York: Hastings House, 1958.

Settle, Mary Lund and Raymond W. *Saddles and Spurs. Saga of the Pony Express*. New York: Bonanza Books, 1955.

Sheldon, Addison E., Ph.D. *Land Systems and Land Policies in Nebraska*. Lincoln: Nebraska State Historical Society, 1936.

Sheridan, General P. H. *Outline of Military Posts. Mili-*

tary Division of the Missouri. Facsimile Reprint. Bellevue, NE: Old Army Press, 1969.

Sorenson, Alfred. *History of Omaha. From the Pioneer Days to the Present Time.* Omaha: Gibson, Miller and Richardson, 1889.

Time Life Books. *The Railroaders.* New York: Time Life Books, 1973.

Ware, Captain Eugene F. *The Indians War of 1864. Being a Fragment of the Early History of Kansas, Nebraska, Colorado and Wyoming.* Lincoln: University of Nebraska Press, 1960.

Webb, Walter Preston. *The Great Plains.* New York: Ginn and Company, 1931.

Wetmore, Helen Cody. *Last of the Great Scouts. The Life Story of Colonel William F. Cody.* Lincoln: Bison Books, 1965.

Wilson, D. Ray. *Fort Kearny on the Platte.* Carpenterville, IL: Crossroads Communications, 1980.

———. *Nebraska Historical Tour Guide.* Carpenterville, IL: Crossroads Communications, 1983.

Yost, Nellie Snyder. *The Call of the Range. The Story of the Nebraska Stock Growers Association.* Denver: Sage Books, 1966.

———. *Buffalo Bill, His Family, Friends, Fame, Failures, and Fortunes.* Chicago: Swallow Press, 1979.

MAGAZINES AND PAMPHLETS

Buecker, Thomas R. "Fort Niobrara, 1880–1906." *Nebraska History,* (Fall 1984):301–325.

———. "Letters of Caroline Frey Winne from Sidney Barracks and Fort McPherson, 1874–1878." *Nebraska History,* (Spring, 1981):1–46.

———. "The Post of North Platte Station, 1867–1878." *Nebraska History,* (Fall, 1982):381–398.

Cook, Captain J. H. "Early Days in Ogallala." *Nebraska History,* (April–June, 1933):83–99.

Haugen, T. Josephine. "The Lynching of Kid Wade." *Nebraska History,* (January–March, 1933):18–34.

Herman, Dick. *Cheyenne County Historical Association Interviews.*

Hytrek, Anthony J. "History of Fort Robinson." (Thesis), 1971.

Interior of the Territory of Nebraska to the East. "Freighting in 1866, a Letter. (January 28, 1866)." Lincoln: Nebraska State Historical Society (1894):44–49.

Mahnken, Norbert R. "Ogallala, Nebraska's Cowboy Capital." *Nebraska History,* (April–June, 1947):85–109.

Nebraskaland Magazine, August, 1981.

Nelson, Vance. "Fort Robinson during the 1880s. An Omaha Newspaperman Visits the Post." *Nebraska History,* (Summer, 1974):181–202.

Nebraska Writer's Project Papers, 1937.

Riley, Paul D. "The Battle of Massacre Canyon." *Nebraska History,* (Summer, 1973):221–249.

Rolfe, D. P. "Overland Freighting from Nebraska City." *Nebraska History,* 10(1902):279–293.

Schubert, Frank N. The Fort Robinson YMCA, 1902–1907. A Social Organization in a Black Regiment." *Nebraska History,* (Summer 1974):165–179.

———. "The Violent World of Emmanuel Stance, Fort Robinson, 1887." *Nebraska History,* (Summer, 1974):203–219.

Sutton, E. S. "Trial and Death of William (Hank) Dodge." *Nebraska History,* (Fall, 1982):412–437.

NEWSPAPERS

Arapahoe Pioneer

Calloway Courier

Chadron Recorder. June 27, 1893, Jan. 18, 1895, Jan. 24, 1895.

Cherry County News. June 15, 1933.

Council Bluffs Chronotype. March 5, 1856.

Crawford Clipper

Crawford Tribune. Sept. 8, 1890; Oct. 9, 1897; Oct. 23, 1897; Dec. 18, 1897; June 26, 1903; Jan. 19, 1906; May 18, 1906; Jan. 25, 1907; Feb. 11, 1911.

Culbertson Progress

Custer County Independent

Custer Leader

Deuel County Herald (Chappell). Nov. 5, 1936

Edgeport Blade. June 1, 1923.

Kearney County Gazette

Kearney Hub. Dec. 24, 1932.

Keith County News (Ogallala). Feb. 19, 1886; July 27, 1922; Aug. 3, 1922; Aug. 10, 1922; Aug. 17, 1922; July, 1976.

Lincoln County Advertiser (North Platte). Oct. 2, 1872.

Lincoln Evening Journal

Lincoln Star. March 31, 1936; June 23, 1936.

Lodgepole Express. Oct. 23, 1919.

Merna Record

Missouri Democrat. May, 1867.

Nebraska Advertiser (Brownville). Aug. 13, 1857; April 15, 1858; Jan. 20, 1859; June 2, 1859; Dec. 13, 1860; May 23, 1862; April 7, 1864; June 17, 1864; July 7, 1864; Aug. 16, 1866; Nov. 18, 1869; March 17, 1870; June 30, 1870; March 20, 1873; Sept. 11, 1882.

Nebraska City News. March 7, 1857; March 28, 1857; April 3, 1858; June 5, 1858; June 11, 1859; June 25, 1859; May 11, 1867; Sept. 11, 1882.

Nebraska Herald (Plattsmouth). Oct. 17, 1867; Oct. 24, 1867; Feb. 20, 1868.

Nebraska State Journal (Lincoln). March 31, 1890; Jan. 18, 1895; Aug. 7, 1896; Dec. 19, 1896; Dec. 17, 1899; March 16, 1900; June 16, 1900; July 19, 1900; March 3, 1904; Nov. 10, 1908; July 2, 1909; Oct. 7, 1909; June 21, 1911; June 25, 1911; Aug. 2, 1911; Sept. 10, 1911; Oct. 17, 1911; Nov. 22–Dec. 8, 1914; Oct. 15, 1915; March 7, 1916; July 29, 1916.

North Platte Enterprise

North Platte Republican. July 10, 1875; Nov. 6, 1875; April 8, 1876; April 15, 1876; June 17, 1876; July 29, 1876; July 12, 1879; Oct. 15, 1881.

North Platte Telegraph. Sept. 1, 1873. Sept. 17, 1873; Jan. 22, 1936.

Ogallala News. Aug. 16, 1937; Dec. 28, 1938.

Omaha Arrow. Nov. 10, 1854.

Omaha Center Agriculturalist. May 14, 1879.

Omaha Daily Bee. Oct. 1, 1879; 1899.

Omaha Daily Nebraskan. July, 1857.

Omaha Weekly Bee. Sept. 11, 1878; Feb. 8, 1882; Sept. 19, 1883; Oct. 12, 1883; Nov. 7, 1883.

Omaha Herald. March 11, 1880; Feb. 8, 1884; June 10, 1884; Aug. 6, 1967.

O'Neill Frontier

Pawnee Republican. Nov. 4, 1880.

The Republican (Valentine). Oct. 15, 1915; March 10, 1916.

Ravenna News. Aug. 26, 1932.

Sidney Enterprise. Sept. 28, 1922.

Sidney Telegraph. March 11, 1880; Jan. 8, 1881; Feb. 8, 1924; June 19, 1951.

Trenton Register. Sept. 25, 1891.

Valentine Democratic Blade

Valentine Reporter

Western Nebraskan (North Platte). Jan. 8, 1875; Jan. 15, 1875; Jan. 22, 1875; Aug. 21, 1875; Sept. 25, 1875; Dec. 4, 1875; July 15, 1876; July 29, 1876; June 1880.

Index